FRANK BRIDGE
— RADICAL AND CONSERVATIVE

Frank Bridge—drawing by Marjorie Fass

Frank Bridge
— radical and
conservative

Anthony Payne

Thames Publishing
14 Barlby Road, London, W10 6AR

© 1984 Anthony Payne

Published in conjunction with the
Frank Bridge Trust

ISBN 0 905210 25 5

PRINTED IN GREAT BRITAIN BY
THE EASTERN PRESS LIMITED
LONDON AND READING

Contents

Frank Bridge: A prelude   *page*   8
I.   The early chamber music   12
II.   The first orchestral works   24
III. The middle period   39
IV.   Years of transition   48
V.   Final harvest   71
VI.   The final orchestral works   98

Index   109
The Frank Bridge Trust   111

Illustrations — pages 49–52 and 61–64

FRANK BRIDGE
— radical and conservative

A prelude

I: The Early Chamber Music

Bridge's unique stylistic journey — combination of German and French elements — growing mastery of first decade, but little emotional growth — command of abstract musical processes — influence of Cobbett's phantasy competitions — *Phantasy String Quartet* — *Phantasy Piano Trio* — *Phantasy Piano Quartet* — *First String Quartet*, early spaciousness of Bridge's thought — command of string sonority and stylistic pointers to the future in *Noveletten* and *Idylls* — *Piano Quintet*, Bridge's problems with development — *String Sextet* — the phantasy 'arch' form as a revelation of the essence of Bridge's vision.

II: The First Orchestral Works

The perspective of Bridge's first period not essentially changed by his orchestral music — *The Sea* combines evocative poetry with clear musical processes — *Isabella* — *Suite for Strings*, technical perfection allied to deep feeling — admirable quality of early work to some extent mitigated by suave predictability, lack of contrast and symphonic engagement — Bridge's realisation of his one-dimensional thinking — comparison of *Dance Rhapsody* and *Dance Poem* — *Dance Poem's* pointers to the future, a transitional achievement, increasing chromaticism, a more flexible thematicism.

III: The Middle Period

A ripening sensibility revealed in 'English' romanticism of *Summer* — growing complexity of feeling in *Two Poems* — *Second String Quartet*, Bridge's first undoubted chamber masterpiece, motivic saturation of texture, overall thematic integration — *Cello Sonata* — Bridge opens himself up to increased range of influences, including Holst — *A Prayer*.

IV: Years of Transition

Developing language associated perhaps with trauma of the Great War, a cultural tradition destroyed — *Christmas Rose*, an operatic nativity play — brief survey of short piano pieces focuses Bridge's electicism — exploration of various styles and manners — difficulty of reconciling demands of amateur market with the increasingly radical language — *songs* surveyed — disappearance of miniatures from Bridge's output — *Piano Sonata* shows full force of Bridge's changing style, determined bitonality, tragic and bitter feeling.

V: Final Harvest

Third String Quartet establishes total break with the past, relates to Second Viennese School while retaining a strong personal tone — *There is a willow* explores twilight world typical of late-Bridge — *Enter Spring*, formal proportions not entirely successful but proves the late style capable of a brighter vision, recalls earlier 'English' manner — darker forces prevail in *Trio Rhapsody*, *Second Piano Trio*, a completely individual masterpiece, and *Violin Sonata* — A new classicism and gritty optimism mark *Fourth String Quartet*, one of Bridge's greatest works, and perhaps his most radical — *Divertimenti* confirm Bridge's classical trend.

VI: The Final Orchestral Works

Phantasm, a flawed conception but presents an English expressionist vision for which there are no precedents — *Oration*, perhaps Bridge's masterpiece, a monumental funeral adress over the dead of the Great War — *Rebus*, Bridge's last complete work, establishes a new simplicity of form and language — unfinished *Symphony for Strings* leaves enigmatic impression — tragedy of Bridge's untimely death prevents him from establishing contact with the young post-war progressives — a figure who reconciled an advanced European language with an English vision.

Frank Bridge: A prelude

When, in 1973, I wrote the two articles about Frank Bridge for *Tempo* which in an extended form were to become an earlier version of this book, surprisingly little of his music was known. Many scores were unavailable, major works were still unpublished, and only a handful of commercial recordings existed of his music. Compared with that of his English contemporaries, Bridge's music was in a state of shameful neglect. My own interest had been aroused by isolated BBC broadcasts during the 1960s of works like the *Fourth Quartet*, the orchestral piece *Summer*, and the marvellous tone-poem for chamber orchestra *There is a Willow Grows Aslant a Brook*. Finally, I had been bowled over by Britten's performances of *Enter Spring*, isolated events which marked the rediscovery of a major orchestral score formerly thought to have been lost: such was the haphazard world of Bridge performance, production and scholarship at that time.

Inevitably my own first estimate of the music was based on a far from complete knowledge. A key work like *Phantasm* had to be assessed from a two-piano score, and I was compelled to form my high opinion of *Oration* — a work that still seems to me to be Bridge's masterpiece — without any acquaintance with the live sound, since it had not apparently been performed for 25 years and no recordings, private or otherwise, could be traced.

The reasons for this sad state of affairs were not far to seek. Bridge's increasingly modernistic tendencies during the 1920s and 1930s quickly lost him the sympathetic audience and critical responses his easier-going early style had won, and by the time he died in 1941 his star had been eclipsed. The war prevented those memorial activities and reappraisals which might have followed the event in easier times, and by the end of hostilities Bridge's fate had been sealed. Traditionally-minded listeners, in tune with the music of the composer's more conservative contemporaries, remained indifferent, while the newer generation of music lovers, who had not had the opportunity to become acquainted with the radical later works, were largely unaware of this fascinatingly cosmopolitan Englishman, an artist who if the fates had been kinder could have stood as father-figure to the young post-war progressives.

For over 20 years the situation remained largely unchanged. Perform-ances and broadcasts were very few and far between, and only the most persevering enthusiast could have gained anything like a coherent picture of Bridge's achievement. An honourable exception was provided by Bridge's famous pupil Benjamin Britten, who made sure that the name of his old teacher and friend did not totally disappear. One can be sure that it was more than a sense of duty that prompted Britten's activities, but the effect, ironically, was merely to remind us who Britten's teacher was, as it was also in the case of the many performances of his own *Variations on a theme of Frank Bridge*. Meanwhile, the work of such contemporaries as Bax, Ireland and Moeran was being thoroughly explored by the record companies and by BBC Radio — a whole book could be written about the sub-culture of those many music-lovers whose favourite works exist on disc and tape and never receive concert performance; it would reveal fascinating cultural patterns which our stereotyped concert programmes do nothing to reflect.

One would like to think that the sheer quality of Bridge's work made a resurgence of interest in it inevitable, quite apart from the absorbing historical aspects of his stylistic development; but whatever the factors involved, his music was certainly heard with increasing frequency during the 1970s, supported by certain record companies, the BBC, and latterly the work of the Frank Bridge Trust. At the present time of writing, in fact, no-one need be ignorant of the basic outlines of Bridge's creative achievement, and those wishing to explore more deeply will find virtually all the major works available on disc and in score, whether they be early or late in style. As a consequence I have been able to take the opportunity offered by the publication of a new version of this book to expand its scope in order to cover pieces which I could not have known ten years ago, and to modify certain opinions about works which I had not had the time to come to know in depth. Now that I have lived with much of Bridge's music for nearly ten years, my feelings for it have been subjected to the inevitable processes of growth and transformation. A few weaknesses which I had suspected earlier, but was unwilling to make too much of in view of my still comparatively slight acquaintance, now seem more obvious to me. Alternatively, music which I was originally only mildly enthusiastic about now seems to be standing the test of time more successfully than I had suspected it would. Interestingly it is the early Edwardian and 'English' late-romantic, middle-period works that have yielded increasingly reward-ing experiences, while certain of the radical late works have come to seem at least in part flawed.

9

My sympathy for the music of Bridge's earliest creative period, which to an initially prejudiced ear had sounded a little tired in language and feeling, began to grow after hearing the *Suite for Strings*, a work I had not known when writing the first version of this book. Here was music of captivating poetry, deeply serious and vivaceous by turns, wonderfully imagined and most elegantly crafted for the medium, yet wearing its compositional science lightly. Like much by Bridge its power to move did not fully reveal itself immediately, the elements of discretion and privacy are always strong in his work; but further hearings made it increasingly clear that the suite possessed quite special qualities, as freshly communicative now as on the day the music was written. Subsequently I began to hear other pieces from the same period with a more enlightened ear, not expecting other than what they were capable of giving. An extra door to the music, and indeed to my own musical unconscious, had been opened, and works like *The Sea*, the *First Quartet* and the *Idylls* and *Novelletten* began to glow in the listening mind much as they originally must have done.

Bridge had achieved by the end of his first creative period a perfection of utterance and a technical deftness, albeit alligned to a limited area of feeling, which few composers would be disposed to dismiss lightly, yet shortly afterwards he gave notice that he was not to be the kind of artist to settle in a stylistic or emotional rut and endlessly cultivate the same territory. He showed that he had the courage — and not all creative artists possess this particular brand of courage — to experiment with style in response to new perceptions and risk a period of less successful creativity before achieving a new perfection. The *Dance Poem* of 1913 furnishes us with an early example of this sort of writing, and it established a pattern of creative behaviour which was to have lasting repercussions. It involved a willingness to place integrity of personality at risk, by identifying with other styles: Holst to some extent in mid-career, Scriabin, Berg and others later. If this eclectic flexibility produced certain works which seem less sure of their course and personality, marking the cross-roads on his developmental path, the ultimate gain in personality growth and poetic richness provides more than ample compensation.

The conservative nature of the musical society Bridge found himself working in between the wars made his task the more difficult, involving as it did stylistic allignments and developments with which most of his contemporaries, professional and otherwise, seem to have been totally out of sympathy. We know that he felt the pressures keenly, especially, for instance, in the sometimes savagely uncomprehending reviews he received; and the need to communicate, which his early music proves to have been a strong element in his character, must have led him constantly to re-examine his stylistic position and to regret the dwindling audience for his work. The artistic path for such a man, torn between vision, the need for inner growth to express itself, and the duty of a professional composer in society, is hard indeed. Added to this adverse artistic climate was the poor health that dogged the final ten years of his life, a time when he might have been expected to forge ahead after establishing a radically original style in the splendid achievements of the previous five years. All in all this was not a settled or particularly happy time for Bridge and I think we may safely say that he was prevented from realising his full potential because of it. Composing time and creative momentum were lost at an absolutely crucial stage in his career, and we lack what would have surely been an impressive and challenging final period in his life's work, something which his comparatively sporadic output over the final years can only hint at.

The early chamber music

Bridge's unique stylistic journey — combination of German and French elements — growing mastery of first decade, but little emotional growth — command of abstract musical processes — influence of Cobbett's phantasy competitions — *Phantasy String Quartet* — *Phantasy Piano Trio* — *Phantasy Piano Quartet* — *First String Quartet*, early spaciousness of Bridge's thought — command of string sonority and stylistic pointers to the future in *Noveletten* and *Idylls* — *Piano Quintet*, Bridge's problems with development — *String Sextet* — the phantasy 'arch' form as a revelation of the essence of Bridge's vision.

The neglect of Frank Bridge's music by performers and writers since his untimely death in 1941 has delayed a full examination of one of the most fascinating developments of style and personality in 20th-century English music. It is the record of an artist's slow recognition of his deepest self, after a leisurely decade of reasoned creative work in which he does not seem to have felt the need to explore the deeper recesses of his personality, or more probably found it impossible to face such dark sources of inspiration and revelation, and temporarily suppressed them. It was only after a long period of emotional and intellectual development that his rich and complex character proved capable of revealing itself, enabling Bridge to balance his rational and orderly flow of ideas with a dark, irrational fantasy. Possibly the experience of the war marshalled the hidden forces in Bridge's nature, and forced him to come to terms with them. But even without such a catalyst his enquiring mind, always alert to the development of style and language, might have led him on to self-discovery by means of technique. Certainly the music prior to his unexpectedly radical development in the 1920s is of slowly increasing depth and individuality.

From the outset of his career Bridge had possessed an exceptionally fluent and logically ordered technique stemming from 19th-century German methods and tempered by a Gallic clarity and lightness. Unlike his many British contemporaries who had received a similar German-based grounding in composition, he does not seem to have questioned its premises. No antidote was required to the prescribed manner of thematic argument, functional harmony and tonal architecture, as it was in the case of Holst, Vaughan Williams, Ireland and others. This factor accounts for the difference between his music and that of, say, Bax and Ireland, with whom he shared (at least until the middle 1920s) more than a few turns of phrase and harmony. The vocabulary might have been similar, but hardly the syntax. This cast of thought enabled him later to assimilate elements of Bergian expressionism, and alienated him from a public more used to British composers whose modernism was tinged with Debussy, Ravel or Stravinsky.

If Bridge's Germanic predilections arose from the Brahmsian training of his teacher Stanford, his early language is certainly not slavishly imitative. It rarely sounds like Brahms, and a personal identity, although as yet pale in outline, is nearly always evident. In the touching innocence of its romanticism there is no trace of foreboding, no premonition that the innocence will one day be destroyed. Texturally the composer it most often calls to mind is Fauré — the Fauré of the *Piano Quartets* and the First *Violin Sonata*, where the vestiges of a Brahmsian influence are likewise being dissolved. There is the same easy flow of ideas, and in the works for piano and strings — the *Phantasy Quartet, Phantasie Trio* and *Piano Quintet* — the same method of supporting mellifluous string polyphony with simple keyboard figures, often arpeggiated.

None of the works from the period 1906 – 1912 shows an unusual advance in emotional scope or individuality over its predecessors. One can point to signs of an increasing structural richness and technical mastery, but to talk in general terms about both the technique and emotional scope, say, in the five major chamber works of the period is not to misrepresent them, since they all explore the same restricted territory. On the other hand, the fluency of thought and the ingenuity of structure and thematic working are remarkable, and show Bridge to have been a master of purely musical discourse at a time when the pre-occupations of many of his British contemporaries were mystical and poetically atmospheric. In fact abstract music occupies a dominating position in his output, although he also contributed examples of nature music and tone poetry which were the equal of anything of the kind written at that time.

One of the most important influences upon Bridge's evolution of personal structural principles was the series of chamber-music competitions organised by W W Cobbett. Cobbett had the stimulating idea of forging a link with the great Elizabethan and Jacobean age of English chamber music by setting up competitions for single-movement, so-called 'phantasies'. He thus did something to combat the automatically accepted four-movement archetype, encouraging a fresh approach to the principle of unity in diversity with a movement that would embrace the contrasting

13

tempos and textures of classical precedent by means of thematic interconnexion.

In Bridge's case this stimulated an all-important approach to form which remained with him throughout his career. Three of his early chamber pieces were entered for Cobbett's competitions: the *Phantasie String Quartet* (1901), the *Phantasie Piano Trio* (1907) — which took a first prize — and the *Phantasy Piano Quartet* (1910). The arch-shaped structures he invented in these works cast long shadows: even in pieces which are not in one movement, the phantasy idea can be seen at work, producing in, for instance, the later Cello Sonata, a second movement which combines *adagio* and *finale*.

One of the most radical developments of the principle occurs in the *Rhapsody Trio* for two violins and viola of 1928 (although *Rhapsody* is a misleading term for this bitingly concentrated single movement), while the grandest can be heard in what is perhaps Bridge's masterpiece *Oration*. In still subtler relationship to the phantasy arch-form is Bridge's tendency to return to the opening of a work during the closing pages, even when a three-movement layout has been employed, as in the Piano Quintet or the Fourth String Quartet.

The three Phantasies themselves, however, are uncomplicated examples of formal integration for all their effectiveness. Indeed, the *Phantasy String Quartet* is little more than a short traditional structure in which the three movements are connected by rudimentary links, although it does exhibit some of the characteristics that made the phantasy so important for Bridge's subsequent development: arch-shaped sonata form is used in the opening and closing movements, in which the recapitulation of second-subject material precedes that of the first, and there is moderate recourse to first-movement material in the finale. The two later works show an increasing refinement of form and language, however, and the schemes involved, the *Phantasy Piano Trio*'s A (allegro moderato) — B (andante) — C (scherzo) — B — A, and the *Phantasy Piano Quartet*'s A (andante) — B (allegro) — C (trio) — B — A, suggest the variety of possibilities offered by the form. Both works open with a dramatic challenge and then proceed to a leisurely unfolding of the principal melodic material. In the Trio the subject is stated over an ostinato on the piano which persists for 46 bars (*Ex 1b*). This is typical of the simplicity of Bridge's keyboard writing; and typical, too, is the way the melody moves forward in easy-going periods with a leisurely counter-statement leading to the dominant and to subsequent polyphonic growth.

On paper the repetitive rhythms and the simple modulations may seem naive; but even with such basic material, Bridge already possessed a sense of the broad paragraph which carries the listener easily forward. The *Andante* proceeds by analogy to an easy counter-statement and subsequent imitative sequences, and the climax, typifying Bridge's judgment in the placing of events, comes only after the intervening *Scherzo*.

An important aspect of the Trio's motivic work and transformation is first defined by the dramatic prelude (*Ex 1a*). The following example shows how x generates the opening melodic span (*Ex 1b*), then invades what by now seems to be an independent line (*Ex 1b*), and how later the

Ex. 1c

two components x and y interact to produce a further release of lyrical energy (*Ex 1c*).

The *Phantasy Piano Quartet*, which comes at the end of what might be called Bridge's first period, shows how he had developed mastery and assurance without really enlarging his expressive range. The initial melodic span still uses the textbook harmonic vocabulary that perhaps seems a little faded today, while the melody avoids disjunct shapes and chromatic inflections (*Ex 2a*). The supple phrasing, however, is Bridge at his most inventive; and when the counter-statement leads, as in the *Trio*, to expansive polyphonic extensions, we reach one of those heart-warming

Ex. 2a

16

Ex. 2b

sequences which are the hallmark of the composer's early manner. The easy contrapuntal mastery with which motive x in *Ex 2b* flows in imitation through beautifully judged modulations can indeed be related to Brahms, different though the sound-world is. The arrival of F major at the end of the example creates a fine sense of elevation, and initiates further lovely melodic growths. Very characteristic of Bridge's harmony at this time are the chromatic sixths in *Ex 2b* — the nearest he gets in his early music to using harmony for sensuous effect rather than as part of the linear argument.

Although the *Phantasy Piano Quartet* shows early Bridge at his finest, two other works approach it in craftsmanship and breadth: the First String

17

Quartet and the String Sextet. The Quartet, named the *Bologna* following its success there in a competition in 1906, is the composer's first large-scale work of real identity, and it brings to a peak his early preoccupation with the string quartet medium, capitalising on the experience gained from writing the Phantasy String Quartet (1905), and the two sets of salon pieces, *Novelletten* (1904) and *Idylls* (1906). It is a work that tells us much about the newly emergent composer, an exceptionally adroit craftsman for a 25-year-old at this period in English music, yet also cautious in what he expects of his players and listeners. There is a revealing lack of those knotty incidents in melody and texture which would suggest the young composer coming to grips with an individual vision. We can perhaps conclude that Bridge was the type of artist whose creative personality was initially founded on a natural gift for composition and a strong feeling for good taste, rather than on a burning sense of his own uniqueness as a human being. That was only to develop later.

Bridge's skill was in advance of all his contemporaries at this time, but his first consideration was accessibility and practicality — admirable tenets if harnessed to pressure of vision, but dangerous when given over-riding importance, compelling the composer to use familiar tags, explore well-charted emotional territories, and smooth all corners and edges. In this way growth can be hindered, and it is not surprising that some saw the composer as 'too professional' in his methods. Luckily for his art, Bridge later developed a strong curiosity about styles and techniques outside his immediate world, and allowed his growing store of emotional experience to connect with his compositional mastery; but this is not prefigured in his early music.

Despite these considerations, however, the First Quartet, judged on its own merits, is still an admirable achievement. The slow movement, a 'song without words', and the gracious *scherzo* and *trio* are redolent of Bridge's salon style, but the opening sonata structure announces the composer's wider aims. It was a mistake, perhaps, to treat the easy-going second subject at length in the development prior to extending it even further during the recapitulation, but the evolution of new material at fig 11 by combining first- and second-subject motives marks a real structural achievement, and the spaciousness of the movement as a whole shows Bridge's early sense of musical architecture. This, rather than the invention of immediately memorable individual incidents, was always to be the main embodiment of his thought. Both the intervallic content of the opening theme, for example, and its rhythmic outline prove to be motivically fruitful, and already we find first-movement material clinching paragraphs in the third and fourth movements, a characteristic unifying process.

By their very nature the *Noveletten* and *Idylls* could not play as big a part in the growth of Bridge's command over structural forces, but they were vital to his artistic development in other respects. There is, for example, great technical flare and originality in the writing for strings, especially in matters of textural spacing and colour, and the airy, high-lying brilliance of the third novelett's introduction sounds a daring and authoritative note unusual for its period. How this must have resounded in Britten's mind, not to speak of the second *Idyll*, which supplied the theme for his *Variations on a Theme of Frank Bridge* and which, more importantly from Bridge's point of view, hints for the first time in its private, almost Viennese chromaticism at the composer's ultimate point of arrival. All of this is not to say that the miniature forms of these pieces preclude serious development: the mysterious opening of the first Novelett, poetically evocative in its own right, also plants tonal seeds with its unpredictable harmony which bear fruit in the lyrical unfolding of the main section,

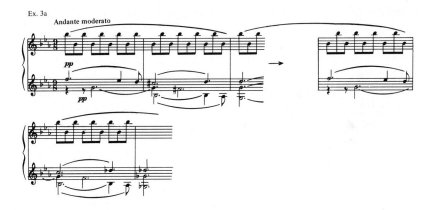

Ex. 3a

(*Ex 3a*). G minor, the first area traversed, proves its importance very shortly afterwards, (*Ex 3b*), and G flat a little later (*Ex 3c*); while the main section's little punctuating figure (*Ex 4a*) states the dominants of these two regions and later develops the idea (*Ex 4b*). The coda resolves the tonal stress by making a feint at the initial G minor progression before moving through it to the home tonic, and then by encompassing the flatter region through a subtle re-allignment of the voice leading in the final

19

Ex. 3b

Ex. 3c

Ex. 4a

Ex. 4b

20

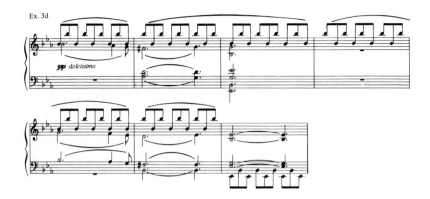

cadence (*Ex 3d*). Prophetic, too, is the arch-shaped sonata form of the finale — this before Bridge's first phantasy — also the references to the second movement in that movement's short development, and to the first in its recapitulation.

Less far-reaching but nonetheless significant craftsmanship transforms the first *Idyll*'s simple ternary design into a touching emotional journey. The sombre C sharp minor opening produces a tender continuation in E warmed by parallel 6 – 3 chords (*Ex 5a*), and in the central episode a

Ex. 5a

Adagio molto espressivo

transformation in the tonic major, retaining the 6 – 3 chords and the chromatically falling major triads, but elaborating the top line, moves deeper into nostalgic radiance, checked only by the cello's insistent reminder of the main section's triplets (*Ex 5b*).

21

Ex. 5b

Two other chamber works date initially from this time, both texturally and formally more ambitious, but they were extensively reworked towards the end of what we can see as Bridge's first creative period: the *Piano Quintet* (1904 – 12) and the *String Sextet* (1906 – 12). Despite benefitting from the ministrations of a more experienced technique, the *Quintet* is not as successful as the *First String Quartet* or the *Piano Trio* and *Piano Quartet*. The original version of the work is still in existence, and comparison with the published score shows that Bridge completely rewrote the development sections of the first and last movements, and drawing on his phantasy experience replaced the middle section of the slow movement with music from the scherzo. It is evident from this that Bridge was aware of problems in the writing of development music. In his phantasy structures they are avoided, since contrasting movements are inserted inside each other at the points where genuine sonata development might be expected. When in other works a development proper is attempted, the results too often resemble expository music, lacking the tonal instability which makes for a dramatic journey to the home tonic, and also the contrasted subjects needed for an analogous thematic process. The working-out sections of the *First Quartet* go some way towards finding a convincing solution to the problem, but the revised developments in the *Piano Quintet* still lack variety, purpose and achievement. In the first movement, for instance, the music remains becalmed for a while, a convincing process, learned perhaps from Fauré, but from then on interest flags as stormy gestures are repeated in mechanical sequences, leading to a lyrical unfolding which is rather too like processes in the exposition. Calm is reinstated, but there has been no convincing tonal or thematic crisis to justify it, and after a foreshortened recapitulation of the first subject we return once more and with even less justification to relaxed material. In fact there is a disappointing lack of cohesion and tension after what has been a rather fine exposition, typical of the best early Bridge.

22

The *String Sextet* is a more impressive achievement in nearly all respects, and brings Bridge's first period of chamber music composition to a fitting conclusion. As so often in the composer's earlier music, the two main subjects of the first movement are similar in mood and profile, but melodic extensions and transitional material provide moments of contrast and increased energy to break up the easy flow. Similarly, just when the smooth lyrical unfolding of the development section threatens to saturate the texture, a vigorous fugato is launched, unusually for Bridge, which braces the music at exactly the point where his earlier sonata movements had shown a tendency to flag. Finally, the sonata arch is clinched with an impressive reharmonisation of the main theme. The work's high-point is reached with the deeply felt lament of the *Andante*, whose grief-filled repetitions find ideal contrast in the restless energy of a central *scherzo*. This movement marks a distinct improvement over the similar 'phantasy' structure in the *Piano Quintet*, whose lyricism is rather vacuous in its serenity and fails, despite a well-planned climax after the intervening *scherzo*, to achieve incandescence. In the finale, Bridge makes his most determined attempt so far at thematic integration, developing first- and second-movement themes along with the finale's own material, and combining its second subject with that of the first movement in the recapitulation.

This use of arch-forms and of pervading thematic integration — devices which have been associated with the Cobbett competitions, although we know that Bridge was thinking along these lines before writing his first phantasies — reveals what is perhaps the single most important fact about his creative mind. His was not a vision of drama, conflict and dynamic progress, rather of lyrical unfolding in closed forms; hence his tendency to remove the first-subject repeat to the end of the movement, lessening the dramatic impact of the reinstatement of the home key, which was now associated with more relaxed material, and transforming the first subject's appearances into the static foundations of an arch where traditionally they had formed dynamic events on a musical journey. The use of thematic integration can be seen as a compensation for the lack of a purposefully dramatic sonata progress, just as in its different way it was for the Second Viennese School.

The first orchestral works

The perspective of Bridge's first period not essentially changed by his orchestral music — *The Sea* combines evocative poetry with clear musical processes — *Isabella* — *Suite for Strings*, technical perfection allied to deep .feeling — admirable quality of early work to some extent mitigated by suave predictability, lack of contrast and symphonic engagement — Bridge's realisation of his one-dimensional thinking — comparison of *Dance Rhapsody* and *Dance Poem* — *Dance Poem's* pointers to the future, a transitional achievement, increasing chromaticism, a more flexible thematicism.

This picture is not essentially altered by the orchestral works of the period — *Isabella* (1907), *Dance Rhapsody* (1908), *Suite for Strings* (1908) and *The Sea* (1910–11) — although the range of instrumental colour available in, say, *The Sea* encouraged him to emphasise sensuousness of texture as an embodiment of visual and poetic imagery, which adds an expressive dimension missing from the chamber music. Perhaps Bridge's characteristic quality of pure musical discourse recedes a little in perspective as a result, but thematicism, clarity of line and structural proportion are still of prime importance in *The Sea*, and in harnessing these qualities to an evocative nature poetry Bridge produced the crowning achievement of his early period.

The first of its four movements, for instance, entitled *Seascape*, exposes one of those shapely themes in compound time typical of early Bridge. It unfolds lazily with a characteristic counterstatement and majestic harmonic progressions until increasing intensity through canonic elaboration builds to a climax (*Ex 6a* and *b*). The effect is uncannily like the calm swelling of the ocean, and the music continues to flow in stately paragraphs, varying and extending the opening material, punctuated by increasingly turbulent and elaborate presentations of the crowning wave of *Ex 7*. This is music of lyric expansion rather than symphonic engagement, and essentially it remains so even in the violent storm finale, where ideas from the calm opening seascape are transformed by distortion —

Ex. 6a

Ex. 6b

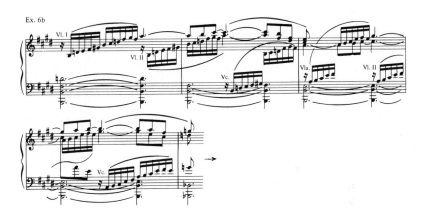

Ex. 6c

25

a musical re-enactment of the process of the elements. The crowning wave of *Ex 7* becomes the howling cry of *Ex 8a* and later the uncanny stillness of *Ex 8b*, the peacefully flowing chains of quavers (*Ex 6b*) becomes a churning chromatic undertow (*Ex 8a*), the main theme (*Ex 6a* and *b*) is stretched out before the driving headwind (*Ex 9*), while on top of all there is a new theme, first presented with its constituent phrases broken by the storm (*Ex 10a*) and finally as an integrated line riding the flood at climax

Ex. 9

Ex. 10a

27

Ex. 10b

and inducing calm — another compelling nature image (*Ex 10b*). The two inner movements, *Seafoam* and *Moonlight*, do not form part of this bigger process, but each is a delightful genre piece. *Moonlight* relies almost entirely on the cool, evocative beauty of its main theme, which returns three times in varied colours but with unchanging harmony. These hypnotically calm paragraphs are linked, as are so many melodic statements in the work, by a punctuating figure which is varied at each appearance. More extended working of the figure at the centre of the movement provides the only contrast to motionless serenity. *Seafoam* is the suite's *scherzo*, and it presents successively a restless semiquaver figure on the strings and a *cantabile* wind theme, before harnessing them in counterpoint with characteristic craftsmanship. The music procedes by rigidly sequential repetitions of four-bar phrases, however, and when the two ideas are combined, revealing identical phrase-structures, the impression becomes increasingly mechanical. A little irregularity and overlapping in the counterpoint might have provided a more genuine feeling of tension by interaction.

Isabella, the earliest of Bridge's extant orchestral pieces, is predictably a little less flexible in structure, but as so often in the music of this period the simple romanticism of the material proves on repeated hearings to possess considerable staying power. It is difficult at first to see how Bridge could have identified with the Keats narrative poem on which the music is founded. Isabella falls in love with her brothers' dependant, Lorenzo. The brothers disapprove, lure him to a forest ride, and murder and bury him. Isabella weeps and awaits him in vain, until a vision reveals the awful deed; whereupon she finds the body and places the head in a pot of basil, only to be robbed of her prize by the vengeful brothers. She died 'imploring for her basil to the last'.

A grisly tale, but it did provide opportunities for purely musical processes which we can see to have been prophetic. There are the separate themes for Isabella and Lorenzo which combine in counterpoint to suggest the couple's loving union (*Ex 11*) — a more fruitful combination this than in *Seafoam* because of the irregular phrasing — and there is the distortion and development in a central allegro of themes heard earlier under happier circumstances to suggest the dark deeds that ended the lovers' bliss (cf, *Seascape* and *Storm*). Where *Isabella* seems formally stiff is in the rather perfunctory transitions between main sections: the narrative seems to provide the link here without musical support. The lyrical growth within the main sections themselves is impressively sustained, however, and if Bridge could have mastered the problem of moving easily from one broad plane of activity to another, as he did in *The Sea* by using developing links, *Isabella* would have been a more impressive achievement.

Dance Rhapsody, to be discussed later in conjunction with *Dance Poem*, exhibits some of the same flaws, but the *Suite for Strings*, dating from the same year, remains one of Bridge's most elegantly composed works. It brings to an orchestral ensemble the command of purely musical thought which distinguishes the chamber music of the period, and it achieves a new technical polish and a depth of feeling which were not to be surpassed for some years. As one would expect from a work of this nature, the emotional territory it explores is an unpretentious one, yet from the very first statement, so exquisitely poised in octaves on violins and violas, one is aware of a seriousness and richness of feeling. The first movement, in fact, is one of Bridge's finest achievements, showing already the influence of the phantasy's arch-formed deployment of themes; and as the work progresses we discover a determined use of thematic transfor-

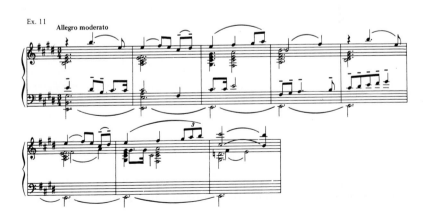

Ex. 11
Allegro moderato

mation and development, drawing even the central movements into an overall integrative process. From this point of view the *Suite* goes even further than *The Sea* in its structural thinking. Something of the effortless growth which it evinces can be seen in Exx 12 and 13. Ex. 12 shows some of the melodic and harmonic growth in the first movement — note, for instance, how the discreet movement to cadence through neapolitan territory at the outset (*Ex 12b*) provokes shortly a more positive neapolitan

Ex. 13a Second movt.
(c.f. First movt. - Ex. 12h)

Ex. 13b

Ex. 13c
Second movt. Trio

f

pizz.

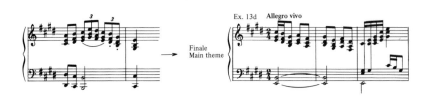

Finale
Main theme

Ex. 13d **Allegro vivo**

Ex. 13e
Adagio molto

Third movt.
(c.f. First movt. Ex. 12d)

pp dolce

Ex. 13f

Ex. 12a

Finale - development
First movt. Ex. 12a & h
Second movt. Ex. 13a
Finale Ex. 13d

p

fp

Ex. 13a

Ex. 13d

Ex. 12h

32

gesture (*Ex 12c*) leading eventually to the movement's magical coda (*Ex 12h*); while Ex 13 indicates some the threads which bind individual movements together. The repertory of English string music from Elgar to Vaughan Williams and Tippett abounds in fine pieces, but it may be safely said that few surpass or even equal Bridge's *Suite*, and the private intensity of its *Nocturne*, a precursor of the deeply felt *Lament for Strings* of 1915, is a most moving experience.

The *Suite for Strings*, *The Sea*, the *Phantasy Piano Quartet* and the *First String Quartet* are all works of considerable attainment; yet towards the end of what we can now see as his first creative period, Bridge seemed to have sensed that something was missing from his music. The fact that he spent much of his time in 1912 reworking two earlier pieces may suggest that he was reviewing his achievement and setting his house in order prior to making important explorations. For all its admirable qualities, the music of this period lacks variety in its tonal and thematic fabric. There is a certain predictability in the suave and usually moderately paced harmonic rhythm, and in the basic similarity of thematic shapes: this means that at the centre of a movement or of a work there is a lack of that engagement of forces which gives big musical structures a sense of power and direction. It is sometimes difficult, for example, to distinguish between expository and developing music because of an overall tonal and thematic stability. Even in *Storm* it is through more active chromatic figuration and more dissonant chord structures that Bridge seeks to paint his scene; the harmonic movement remains slow, the tonality stable, and the ideas follow each other in picturesque succession. Without contrasting material and processes the musical achievement will be considerably diminished, and genuine symphonic thinking will be impossible. Bridge seems to have become increasingly aware of this, realising at about this time that his musical thinking was one-dimensional in its processes and that vital areas of his creative imagination had still to be explored. The subsequent journey towards self-discovery, hastened by the evidently traumatic experience of the First World War, was to lead to a final period of radical activity that set in with startling suddenness at the beginning of the 1920s. But, for the time being, his extension of range depended on no more than a growing intensity in all the aspects of his compositional craft, most significantly in his increasingly elaborate chromaticism.

This development can be studied by comparing two orchestral works whose titles suggest a similarity of aim both artistic and technical, but whose substance marks a growing intellectual scope and emotional

Ex. 14a

leading to

Ex. 14b

Ex. 14c

Ex. 15

34

awareness: the *Dance Rhapsody* of 1908 and the *Dance Poem* composed five years later. The former is an attractive work, full of vigorous invention. But for all its vitality, the achievement is diminished by a rather easy-going approach to the problem of large-scale form. The work consists of a sequence of four contrasted dance sections, only loosely connected by comparatively routine transitions, and it closes with a return to the opening after a brief dominant preparation. That opening is a pounding six-eight, vigorously symphonic in impetus (*Ex 14a, b,* and *c*), but the second section, rather in the manner of an Austrian *schnadahupfler* (*Ex 15*) (was Elgar's first *Bavarian Dance* at the back of Bridge's mind?), and the subsequent *Waltz* (*Ex 16*) and *Polka* (*Ex 17*) sections are more suite-like in treatment. Bridge, out of an innate musicality, ensures a certain overall homogeneity by employing ideas with a family resemblance, even if this only amounts to the similar contours of *Exx 15* and *16*, and the shared head motive of *Exx 15* and *17*. But there is practically no large-scale working of ideas such as we find in the motivically saturated music of his maturity. The only episode that tightens the structural arch and prevents the main body of the work from becoming a casual diversion is a cogent development

Ex. 16

Ex. 17

Ex. 18

of the opening theme which appears in the middle of the *Waltz* (*Ex 18*).

The tuneful, if also naive, quality of invention which characterises the *Dance Rhapsody* has virtually disappeared from Bridge's vocabulary by the time of the *Dance Poem*, and this marks a crucial step forward in his development. In the later work immediately arresting themes are replaced by material whose flexible shapes are designed with a view to motivic transformation and contrapuntal working (*Exx 19a, b, c* and *d*), and the textures are considerably more chromatic (*Ex 19d*). The contrasted modes of thought are epitomised by the boldly rhetorical opening of the *Rhapsody* (*Ex 14a*) and the eliptical assemblage of motives that launches the *Poem* (*Ex 19a*).

The form of the *Poem* is that of a slow symphonic waltz in the by now familiar sonata arch-form, and Bridge provided a programme for the first performance, relating the main sections to a dramatic sequence of balletic situations and moods: Introduction (Dancer) — First Subject (Allurement) — Second Subject (Abandon) — Development (Tenderness) — Recapitulation (Problem) — Coda (Disillusion). The preoccupation with

Ex. 19a

Ex. 19b

Ex. 19c

Ex. 19d

thematic evolution and integration goes some way beyond anything found in Bridge's earlier music, and makes the *Poem* a far more concentrated work than the *Rhapsody*. In attempting a greater unity, however, Bridge failed to provide a sufficiently varied range of ideas, and the similarity between the second subject and the transformation of it which dominates the development makes for monotony at a crucial stage in the work's progress. There should have been a bolder array of transformations: the main theme and that of the central development fit together in easy counterpoint for their combined recapitulation, for instance (*Ex 19c*), but the achievement in harnessing such uneventful shapes is perhaps not that great. There is nevertheless much that is expressively new, as in the coda's haunted gestures: thematic processes in disarray, crescendos breaking off in disillusion, muted trumpet fanfares sounding over an uneasy ostinato — dislocated statements which his earlier style would have been incapable of. In fact, *Dance Poem* is a significant and encouraging work in several respects, offering a glimpse of much broader horizons than the music immediately preceding it.

The middle period

A ripening sensibility revealed in 'English' romanticism of *Summer* — growing complexity of feeling in *Two Poems* — *Second String Quartet*, Bridge's first undoubted chamber masterpiece, motivic saturation of texture, overall thematic integration — *Cello Sonata* — Bridge opens himself up to increased range of influences, including Holst — *A Prayer*.

Four works may be taken as representative of the period in which Bridge began building on the transitional achievement of *Dance Poem*: the tone poem *Summer* (1914 – 1915), *Two Poems* and the Second String Quartet (1915), and the Cello Sonata (1913 – 17).

Summer already seems to inhabit a more intensely imagined world. The way in which gently insistent figures establish at the outset an aura of concentrated poetry is quite new for Bridge, revealing a ripening sensibility. The melodic flow is still leisurely, and the lyrical main subject undergoes the by now familiar counter-statement and polyphonic growth. But, despite the lazy warmth of the work's poetry, there is a new tension beneath the surface, and much of this has to do with the harmonic textures. Bridge has veered away from the serpentine progressions of the *Dance Poem*, which though interesting in their chromatic syntax were also a little anonymous in tone, and has moved towards the pastoral idiom that in varying degrees served so many of his English contemporaries — an idiom in which diatonic dissonance and modality offset chromaticism. Paradoxically, in so doing he managed to tap a deeper and more individual well of feeling, for contact with more harmonically minded composers like Delius, Ireland and Bax greatly enriched a language that had so far concentrated upon developing line and discourse.

Along with this increased harmonic awareness there appear, if only tentatively, juxtapositions of sonority which further the structural arguments, in contrast to the still important melodic and contrapuntal extensions. The orchestral colour-range presumably promoted this tendency or, again, contact with the formal methods of harmonically-dominated composers — for instance, the mosaic of subtly contrasted sonorities in Delius's *In a Summer Garden*. Compared with the highly

39

Ex. 20

unconventional texture-building of Delius, however, Bridge can seem
disconcertingly orthodox to the score-reader. The most resplendent climax
in *Summer*, a paragraph of sustained elevation, reveals part-writing of textbook correctness (*Ex 20*). Nothing could be more characteristic of Bridge
than this perfect marriage between technical orthodoxy and genuinely
original poetic inspiration.

Without disrupting the pastoral serenity that seems to have occupied
Bridge's thoughts at this time, the *Two Poems* for orchestra, which take
as their starting points quotations from Richard Jefferies, embody a more
complex world of feeling. The first uses as its motto 'Those thoughts and
feelings which are not sharply defined, but have a haze of distance and
beauty about them, are always the dearest'. It is an enchanting essay in
evocation and very revealing of Bridge's increasing scope. The emotional
ambivalence behind the hypnotically repetitive harmonic cells (*Ex 21*)

Ex. 21

is, for instance, typical of the composer's mature thought. Does the heart rejoice in rapt contemplation or regret the ultimate transience of things? The gently poised emotion finds an exact analogy in the harmonic ambiguity whereby a delicately sketched bass-line, on harp alone, contradicts the implications of the sustained upper texture. In the middle section we return to a more conventional pastoral manner, the property initially, perhaps, of Butterworth, but the idiom is beautifully handled and assimilated, taking on in context a fresh significance. The second *Poem* is a little *scherzo* and is headed: 'How beautiful a delight to make the world joyous! The song should never be silent, the dance never still, the laugh should sound like water which runs for ever'. The joyful confidence of the writing gives a restrained foretaste of the erruption of similar feelings in *Enter Spring*, and characteristic finger-prints are everywhere to be found, most obviously in the contrapuntal combination of all three main ideas which marks the final climax (*Exx 22, x, y* and *z*).

The seemingly purposeful growth of style which is embodied in *Summer* and the *Two Poems* is not pursued in quite such an orderly fashion by other works from this period. Bridge was capable of looking back as well as forward, and in what was to be the most eclectic stage of his career he also explored modes of thought and execution which were eventually found to be unsuitable and were dropped from his vocabulary.

Bridge's first mature chamber music masterpiece, for example, the Second String Quartet, is more firmly tied to the past than *Summer*, possibly because ideas for the work had germinated over a longer period, or else because the medium encouraged him to rely on the well-tried methods of contrapuntal discourse which were linked to his previous style.

The chromatic language shows a considerable advance over that of the work's predecessors, however, and if the opening subject is related in its smoothly flowing phrases and in the unclouded diatonicism of its top line to Bridge's earlier manner, the tightly organised chromatic part-writing that supports it, although lacking the acute tensions of later years, marks a new complexity of thought (*Ex 23*). There is still a tendency to make spacious and practically unvaried counterstatements — the first movement's second subject is typical — but there is also a new inclination to develop and vary when repeating (*Ex 24*). Again, textures throughout

Ex. 24

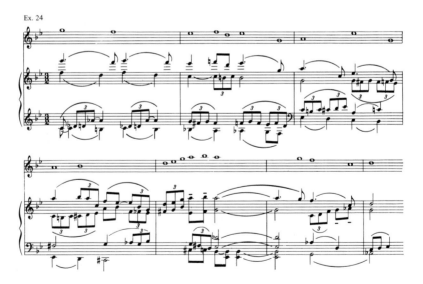

42

Ex. 25a

Ex. 25b

the quartet are motivically saturated in a way that pressages his late style, and thematic evolution and integration are developed to a new pitch. Thus, in the scherzo the insistent triplets of the main subject (*Ex 25a*) evolve new subsidiary themes (*Ex 25b*) which in their turn are transformed into

43

Ex. 25c

the tenderly lyrical andante of the trio (*Ex 25c*), while the finale remains unsurpassed for its preoccupation with by now familiar processes. A wistful *molto adagio* preface which totally transforms the first movement's second subject launches, in a moment of magical sonority, one of Bridge's sonata arch-forms. All the principal themes can be traced back to previous material (*Ex 26*), and the two main subjects are combined in counterpoint immediately before the final coda. This brilliant movement, with its unbroken flood of ideas varied by contrasting colours and textures, represents the kind of music Bridge must have been working towards for years, and the *Second String Quartet* as a whole can be accounted one of the composer's finest achievements.

Ex. 26a

Ex. 26c
1st. movt.
2nd. subject

The period covered by the fourth work under consideration, the Cello Sonata, encompasses that of all the middle-period works so far discussed, and each of the trends discovered there features in it. At every stage in his career Bridge's idiom was particularly well integrated — a mark of his technical fastidiousness and unerring taste — but the Cello Sonata confirms that he was opening himself up to an increasingly wide range of stylistic references at this time. The least nationalistic of composers is found at one point employing the folk-song and organum manner, and, less predictably, responding to the flexible melodic shapes of Rachmaninov. If this latter characteristic is thought to be a mere coincidence in two late-Romantic composers (for Bridge was still this), then the second subject of the Second Quartet's first movement also resembles the other composer in its top line and triplet formations. In the broadest sense, however, the Cello Sonata is pure Bridge throughout. The rolling periods of the opening sonata structure constitute the last of those lyrical flights which were initiated by the Piano Quintet and *Phantasy Trio*; but now the accompaniment fluctuates between support and motivic intrusion which adds richness and tension to the music's progress. The big second movement, which opens with something like a Baxian threnody, develops its chromatic strains with a method and discipline quite unlike that of Bax; and the arch-shaped structure, which incorporates a thematically derived *scherzetto* at the centre, and a strong reference to the work's opening as finale-coda, shows Bridge's formal mastery at its height.

Bridge had now reached a stage in his career where he can be said to have brought his orderly sense of flowing development to a peak. Without breaking with his first-period manner, his textural procedures and melodic writing were acquiring an increased flexibility. He also appeared at this time to be approaching a closer relationship with such composers as Holst and Vaughan Williams. In his only work for chorus and orchestra, *A Prayer*

(1916), he released long sequences of first- and second-inversion triads — a new element in his vocabulary used as extensively as this — while the presence of the chordal motive x in *Ex 27* (cf. *Phantasy Quartet*, y in *Ex 2b*) reminds us of Holst's *Choral Fantasia* — although typically it provides moments of intensity in a flowing paragraph, while in Holst it is a self-sufficient mystical symbol (Ab C E G).

Even more Holstian is the climax at the words 'love to be despised, and not to be known in this world', where the tritonal pull between the pedal G and the upper harmony suggests the other composer's cataclysmic vision (*Ex 28*). The work is in neatly engineered verse form and is clearly tailored for the amateur choir with part-writing that alternates between

Ex. 27

Ex. 28

the simplest note-against-note texture and conventional imitative counter-point. Only in a handful of bars does Bridge abandon four parts for multiple divisions. It could be said, in fact, that the choral writing in both line and harmonic texture is lacking in enterprise. But against this must be weighed its unfailing practicability and effectiveness, and, more importantly, the wider-ranging harmony and colour of the orchestral contribution.

Considering the amount of music that Bridge wrote during the first two decades of the century for amateur performers, whether chamber musicians or vocalists, it is perhaps surprising that he made no further efforts to nourish the most important amateur repertory of all. Certainly a body of choral music in his more approachable style might have helped to sustain his reputation in later years, when his increasingly difficult idiom was not only making the composition of music for amateurs virtually impossible but was also losing him professional patronage.

As yet, however, there were few, if any, indications of the stylistic revolution which lay just ahead, and an informed observer might well have concluded that Bridge was destined to reconcile his cosmopolitan-inclined fluency of thought with the harmonic and textural vocabulary which later generations were to see as typically British. Ultimately, Bridge did indeed effect something of a rapprochement between an English mode of feeling and a broadly-based European language. And yet — for such is the unaccountability of genius — the radical manner in which he achieved it could not have been forseen.

Years of transition

Developing language associated perhaps with trauma of the Great War, a cultural tradition destroyed — *Christmas Rose*, an operatic nativity play — brief survey of short piano pieces focuses Bridge's eclecticism — exploration of various styles and manners — difficulty of reconciling demands of amateur market with the increasingly radical language — *songs* surveyed — disappearance of miniatures from Bridge's output — *Piano Sonata* shows full force of Bridge's changing style, determined bitonality, tragic and bitter feeling.

The development of Bridge's language after the Cello Sonata is so arresting that it suggests some kind of inner upheaval. It was associated, perhaps, with his revulsion against war — Benjamin Britten has spoken of his teacher's passionately held pacifist convictions — and very probably there was also the feeling that his own cultural tradition had disappeared in the holocaust, along with so many lives and hopes, compelling him to forge and feel anew, for the alternative of dreaming over a lost past would have been unthinkable to an artist of Bridge's temperament. On the other hand, his developing language at the time of the Cello Sonata and the Second String Quartet may have unlocked some door to his subconscious. Whatever the case, he appears to have experienced a crisis of style, and perhaps even of personality, immediately after the war. It is significant, for instance, that with one exception no major work seems to have been conceived after the completion of the Cello Sonata until the crucially important Piano Sonata, begun in 1922 but not finished until 1925.

That exception is the little opera in three scenes, *The Christmas Rose*, which was largely sketched in 1919 but not completed and scored until ten years later. It is not clear why Bridge stopped work on the opera when it was, in his own words, three-quarters sketched. Perhaps his growing perception of where his vision would shortly take him prevented him from continuing to work wholeheartedly in a language of middle-period radiance. Or was it that a work launched in euphoric thanksgiving at the cessation of First World War hostilities ran up against a growing retrospective horror, as the composer began to dwell upon what had been lost? Whatever the reason, Bridge only found himself able to complete the work after he had fully explored and mastered his radical late language. He dis-

Frank Bridge

Frank and Ethel Bridge

Bridge (at the piano) with Ethel Bridge (background) and the violinist Antonio Brosa and his wife.

Frank Bridge

covered, no doubt, that the more boyant aspects of this style, which were developed in *Enter Spring* after the darker probings of the Piano Sonata and the Third String Quartet, were not as far removed from his late middle-period work either in technique or feeling as he might previously have suspected they were going to be. But it would be interesting to know whether those passages which seem allied to parts of *Enter Spring* are echoes or pressages. Do they belong to the part that remained to be composed in 1929, or was Bridge already in 1919 so close in at least one aspect to his mature language? If the former, *The Christmas Rose* must be said to mark a high point in the eclecticism which is evident throughout much of Bridge's career, for its wide-ranging material, diatonic, model, polytonal, is integrated to perfection.

For his libretto Bridge turned to a children's play by Margaret Kemp-Welch and Constance Cotterell, which tells how the little son and daughter of one of the Good Shepherds journey to Bethlehem to see the Christ child. It is a musical nativity play rather than a conventional opera and is to be judged as such, concerning itself with miracle and revelation rather than dramatic characterisation. This is not to say that the work is un-stage-worthy: the two children, Miriam and Reuben, are touchingly presented, and the action, though simple, is perfectly suited to the opera's 45-minute span, providing the foundation for a structure whose climaxes are of mystical or visionary intensity.

The opera opens with the vision of the angels bringing tidings of Christ's birth to the three shepherds. The shepherds plan to journey to the manger with gifts, but Miriam, who had been lying awake, also experienced the vision and begs to be taken with them. Her father gently forbids such a dangerous journey, and tells her she must stay and take care of her little brother Reuben. The shepherds depart, and Reuben awakes to be told by Miriam of the angels' message in the only extended solo of the opera. He reminds her that the good tidings were 'for all people', and joyously the two of them depart for Bethlehem in defiance of their parent's orders.

The second scene shows the children tired and lost on the road to Bethlehem — Reuben close to giving up, Miriam thinking that if only he could have shared her vision he would possess the strength to continue. Again the angels are heard, and the children make off with renewed enthusiasm.

The third and final scene opens with the shepherds' arrival at the stable. As they are about to enter, the children appear undetected and, seeing the gifts, realise they cannot follow without offerings of their own. Miriam weeps with disappointment, but as the shepherds reappear and depart, speaking ecstatically of their experience, something begins to stir under the snow. Roses are miraculously springing up where Miriam's tears fell: these are to be their presents, and after an excited duet Miriam and Reuben enter the stable to choral alleluias from the growing crowd of villagers and visitors.

As we have seen, Bridge brought his techniques of thematic transformation and development to a fine peak of poetic sensitivity and structural power during the years immediately preceding the sketching of the opera, and he draws on his full range of resources to outline character and mood, and to unify dramatic structure in the work. The shepherds, for instance, as befits their subsidiary role and generalised presence, are not differentiated. Their pastoral naivity is captured in sequences of parallel unrelated triads, the chords wide-spaced to suggest three characters united by a single experience. It is a motive that can be adapted to all circumstances (*Ex 29*). The children's innocence stands out in more

Ex. 30

How of-ten have you taught me that the Great Messiah ___ would one day come to be our King.

Ex. 31a

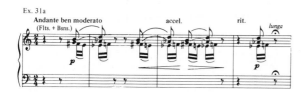

Ex. 31b

O Reu — ben, the King of Glo - ry, de-sired ___ of

all the a — ges, ___ has come down to earth.

Ex. 31c

Some thing is mov - ing un - der -

- neath the snow.

immediately lyrical terms, a contrast to the texture of the shepherds (*Ex 30*), and the theme has a subtle application when suggesting the shepherds' wonder at Christ's lowly birth — how like their own children, they seem to be thinking. This is but one example of the range of associations Bridge draws from his material. An idea associated with tearful disappointment, for instance (*Ex 31a*), is modified when Miriam tells Reuben of the angel's tidings, for her excitement is mixed with sadness at not being able to visit the manger (*Ex 31b*). It finally becomes the bursting rose-buds that spring from Miriam's tears in the last scene (*Ex 31c*). There is also a subtle network of motivic relationships between different themes. The joy of the angels' opening alleluia (*Ex 32a*), which is itself atmospherically developed during Miriam's narration (*Ex 32b*), touches the joyful excitement of the children as they start their journey (*Ex 32c*), and is intimately connected through the motive (x) with the opera's most important and memorable theme, the alleluia or nativity carol representing the Christ child (*Ex 33a*). This melody's deceptively simple ostinato accompaniment of minor sevenths, encompasing the piquant false relation (y), colours the atmosphere of the whole opera, producing, for instance, the evocatively hesitant representation of the

56

Ex. 32a

Ex. 32b

Ex. 32c

57

Ex. 33a

Ex. 33b

If on — — — ly we ⌐, had a gift!

Ex. 34

children's dilemma in the final scene (*Ex 33b*). Again, the impressive fanfare for Christ the king and saviour (*Ex 34*) can be seen to develop the sequence of minor sevenths, stretching them apart while retaining the idea of false relationships — a potent musical symbol.

In contrast, the bright, clear octaves of the guiding star remain immutably fixed in musical space on F sharp, just like the starlight that shines down so steadily, and the chords that emerge from it burn more densely as its meaning becomes more clearly appreciated (*Ex 35*). Fixed, too, is

the E-flat tonality of the lullaby or alleluia, a symbol of unwavering faith and untarnishable innocence, and the centre of tonal gravity in the work's dramatic structure.

That structure, typically, is based on a clear and orderly set of symmetries. Each scene moves dramatically to a point where the children's low spirits turn to excitement and fresh hope in a spirited *allegro*: at the realisation that the tidings are 'for all' in scene i, when the angels' chorus gives them fresh heart in ii, and when the miraculous gift removes the last obstacle to their paying hommage at the manger in iii. There is a range of motives that reappear in varied and developed forms during the passages of disappointment and frustration (C); and the excited *allegros* which they lead up to in Scene i (D) and Scene ii (E) are motivically combined in the equivalent passage of Scene iii. Also, Scenes i and iii begin with passages for the shepherds with their attendant themes (B), and the whole work is enclosed within radiant choruses, 'Glory to God' (A) and 'Alleluia' (F). This produces the broad scheme:

Scene i	Scene ii	Scene iii
A Angels' chorus		
B Shepherds' ensemble		B Shepherds
A Miriam's narration recapitulates angels music		
C The children's disappointment	C The children lost	C Children's frustration.
	(A) Angels heard again	
D Joyful exit	E Fresh hope and joy	D/E Entry into the manger.
		F Chorus: Alleluia.

For the rest, the period between the Cello and the Piano Sonatas was devoted to collections of small piano pieces and a handful of songs, some of which indicate the beginnings of Bridge's new style. At this point it is perhaps worth touching on Bridge's achievements in this field, for to many musicians they are still the only familiar part of his output. The majority of his piano pieces date from the middle period of his career, for the genre, like that of song, became incompatible with his fully developed late style, and they tend to reflect preoccupations which are

A page from Bridge's score of the full orchestra version of 'Sir Roger de Coverley'

Frank Bridge (front right) at a meeting of the Performing Right Society Council

Frank and Ethel Bridge with Bridge's American patroness Mrs Elizabeth Sprague Coolidge (left)

63

Bridge's death-mask

more fully explored in the large-scale works of the period. *Solitude*, for instance, composed in 1913 and published as one of *Three Poems*, obviously relates to the chromaticism of *Dance Poem* in its strangely wandering harmony and line, while *Sunset* (1914), from the same group, pressages the mood of the first of the *Two Poems* for orchestra. Prior to the comparative spate of pieces during this period, which probably stemmed from publishers' growing interest in his music, there were few songs and less piano pieces, suggesting that Bridge was always more concerned with the broader structural arguments than with self-contained statement. The delicious *Three Sketches* for piano of 1906, however, prove his ability in the enclosed world of the character piece: *April* is full of a piquant charm which is untainted by the faded air of much Edwardian salon music, as is *Valse Capricieuse* (which perhaps dates from nearer the publication year, 1915), and *Rosemary* begins with something of the delicacy of a Fauré song, developing a tiny *allegro* in its central episode with unobtrusive yet perfectly judged contrapuntal working. Of the *Three Pieces*, composed mostly in 1912, only *Columbine* recaptures the early charm.

The most prolific years for piano music were 1917 – 18, which saw the composition of the first set of *Miniature Pastorals*, the suite *A Fairy Tale*, the *Four Characteristic Pieces* and the *Three Improvisations* for left hand. The *Pastorals*, beautifully finished, distinctive little pieces for the technically limited, and the suite hold no surprises, but the *Characteristic Pieces* are most arresting, especially in the chromatic piquancy of *Bittersweet* and the impressionism of *Fireflies*, which creates a bitonal whirring out of its appogiatura chords. The *Improvisations* mark a step backwards in idiom, in spite of the vitality of invention in, for instance, *A Revel*, whose little patterns of 5/16 picked out of the triplet semiquaver figuration cause delightful rhythmic cross-currents; and with the exception of the second group of *Miniature Pastorals* (1921), which continues with considerable success the poetic and technical scope of the first set, Bridge's next groups of pieces, *The Hour Glass* and *Three Lyrics*, pursue unpredictable courses. Of the *Three Lyrics, Heart's Ease* (1921) encompasses Bridge's early salon manner, and *The Hedgerow* (1924) something of John Ireland's wistful poetry, while in the humour of *Dainty Rogue* (1922) there is a more typical chromaticism. Clearly the demands of the commercial market were vieing with those inner expressive needs which found a more satisfactory outlet in the Piano Sonata, gestating at the same time. It is perhaps for this reason that the slightly earlier sequence of three pieces, *The Hour Glass* (1920), is better integrated stylistically and possesses a more precisely defined poetic character, whether in the pristine freshness of *The Dew Fairy* or the solemnity of *The Midnight Tide*, with its distant echoes of Debussy's *La Cathédrale Engloutie*.

For all their withdrawn and sometimes melancholy moods, however, these pieces are still recognisably middle-period in style. By the time he was composing the two pieces *Retrospect* and *Through The Eaves*, which comprise *In Autumn* (1924), Bridge's style revolution had really left its mark. In the total, unresolved chromaticism and rich unfamiliar chord formations of the second piece, virtually all in the piano's treble register, we hear an eerie evocation of rustling breezes, dead leaves and creaking rafters, and if *Retrospect* still reminds us a little of John Ireland's brooding, the chromaticism is more determined.

Bridge wrote only a handful of further piano pieces, but they still pursue a wayward stylistic course, and it seems clear that he had no really consistent attitude towards the genre. Not discovering at a deeper level any artistic need to write miniatures, he often seems to have used shorter pieces for the purposes of stylistic exploration, when it was compatible with the demands of the popular market, trying out processes which, if successful, he would return to in a broader context and, if not, discard. *Winter Pastoral* (1928) and *Graziella* (1927), for instance, make elegant concessions to conservative taste without denying the new discoveries, but *Canzonetta* (1927) combines a charming middle-period pastoral with a mechanistically bi-tonal central episode, and makes no attempt to integrate these stylistically disparate elements. This highlights the eclecticism of Bridge's middle years, for it is not usually to be observed operating so baldly within the confines of a single piece. In contrast, *A Dedication* (1928) is stylistically unsullied and calls upon the sonorous bi-tonal harmony of the Piano Sonata's slow movement to great effect, while *Gargoyle* (1928), a piece which remained in manuscript until 1977, strikes out into highly original territory, giving a foretaste of the 'unfeeling' machinery and grotesquerie of parts of the Piano Trio. No less interesting in its different way is *Hidden Fires* (1925), an apparently successful exploration of new ground which was never returned to. Perhaps Bridge became disenchanted with its somewhat over-heated turbulence, but it is a unique essay, and unusually for the composer reveals a world of exclusively pianistic feeling.

There remain the *Vignettes de Marseilles*, a not entirely promising title, given what we know of Bridge's mature vision. They consist of a suite of characteristic impressions composed immediately after a holiday Bridge took in 1925 with his wife and his American friend and patroness Elizabeth

Sprague Coolidge. Although apparently conceived for the piano, they sound more successful in the orchestral transcription which Bridge made of three of them in 1938 under the title *Vignettes de Danse*. It must be admitted that a listener coming fresh to these pieces would find it hard to guess their authorship. There are few positive references to his earlier style, and this itself is interesting for what are little more than diary jottings, while the more atmospheric and exotic aspects of the pieces bear only a distant relationship to the advanced language he was developing in his more serious music at that time. It may well be that the pieces represent a solid attempt to evolve a lighter language compatible with his revolutionary discoveries, but ultimately the results were perhaps not thought worthy of a successor.

For an entirely successful excursion into lighter music, and a particularly witty and joyous one, we must go to the slightly earlier *Sir Roger de Coverley* (1922) for string orchestra (or quartet). This is a splendidly composed diversion in Bridge's chromatic middle-period manner, brilliantly conceived for the medium on which it makes considerable demands. It abounds in capricious humour of an exclusively musical kind, in its counterpoints, and in the delightful feint at the main tune prior to its first complete statement. In the use of *Auld Lang Syne* as a final counter-melody Bridge surely had in mind Holst's brilliant harnessing of the 'Dargason' and 'Greensleeves' in his *St Paul's Suite*. The orchestral arrangements of *Sally in our Alley* and *Cherry Ripe*, composed six years earlier, are similar examples of the genre, and they show a sunny side of Bridge's nature which was to have few, if any, outlets in his final creative period.

In some ways, however, it is perhaps not so surprising that Bridge should have abandoned the lighter side of his music-making at that time. During the first two decades of his career he seems to have been the sort of artist who quite naturally makes concessions to public taste, and was reputedly not the composer, as Cobbett had it, 'to seek to startle or to gain credit (or the reverse) for revolutionary innovations'. Then it was compatible with his easy-going conservatism, but now, from his increasingly radical viewpoint, he must have believed that the simplification required for the amateur market would compromise his artistic integrity.

Much of what has been said of the piano music applies equally to the songs, the composing of which dried up even earlier. The keyboard writing and vocal lines possess all the grace and practicability one expects of Bridge's elegant craftsmanship, but only a handful of items show, in choice of text and musical penetration, the attributes of the committed song composer. All the songs composed before the crucial post-war years belong predictably to the drawing room. But within this potentially stultifying convention, there are achievements like the wryly humourous use of harmonic variation in *So Perverse* (1905) or the ardent impetus of *Love Went A'riding* (1914), which is heightened by impetuous shifts of key, while that quintessentially Edwardian ballad *Go Not, Happy Day* (1903) derives an innocent charm from the crosscurrents of its accompanying sextuplets. There is also a warming flow of lyricism in *Where She Lies Asleep* (1914), which captures something of the lazy tenderness of the contemporary *Summer*, and in *Thy Hand in Mine* (1917) the rapt sequence of diatonic dissonances transforms a rather trite poem. *Strew No More Roses*, on the other hand, characteristically chromatic for its year of composition (1913, the year also of *Dance Poem* and *Solitude*), lacks harmonic vitality.

The post-war years saw the production of several songs of real distinction, possessing the intensity of, say, the best songs of Warlock or Ireland, although none is quite late enough to benefit from Bridge's most concentratedly radical manner. The diatonic dissonance that marked his style for a short period finds a further outlet in the stately Whitman setting *The Last Invocation* (1918), and the next year saw the composition of two of his best songs, the fateful *'Tis But a Week*, whose trampling progress sets 'half a hundred fighting men' in the context of 'the green leaves of May', and *What Shall I Your True Love Tell?*, which sounds a new note of passionate protest in response to Francis Thompson's poem. In contrast, *Into Her Keeping* and the Yeats song, *When You Are Old*, face the ravages of time and loss with a moving serenity.

Bridge's last group of songs belongs to the years of the Piano Sonata, and they share with that work, and the piano pieces contemporary with it, an extreme chromaticism and a restless melancholy spirit. The three Tagore songs, *Dweller In My Deathless Dreams, Day After Day* and *Speak to Me, My Love*, epitomise this transitional period. The rich bi-tonal and chromatic harmonies, often explicable as higher dominant discords, still sometimes distantly recall Ireland, but their greater complexity indicates that Bridge was very close to the stylistic break which he finally achieved in the Third String Quartet. The quality of these late songs makes it regrettable that Bridge did not turn his mind to writing an extended cycle in his mature style. The task would have concentrated his growing command of lyrical immediacy and his long-standing mastery of broad musical structure, as *An Die Ferne Geliebte* did Beethoven's.

The full force of Bridge's creative personality at this crucial time erupted in the Piano Sonata, the work which closed his period of transition and made possible the final late flowering. Its radical procedures began a gradual process of alienation from the public and the performers he had served in pre-war years, but we can now see that it also transformed him from a master craftsman (worthy of admiration, but the author of only one or two works of lasting quality) into a creator of commanding originality and power, the composer of a group of chamber works unsurpassed in 20th-century English music, and of five orchestral works the equal of any of their period by native composers.

What made the Piano Sonata such an extraordinary achievement was the energy and determination with which Bridge withstood the pull of conventional tonal language, and developed logically a bitonal harmonic texture throughout large-scale structures. Several of Bridge's English contemporaries were sooner or later to enjoy the frisson obtained from bitonal aggregations, but generally these procedures only resulted in a temporary blurring of some unambiguous tonal outline and were simply a form of chromatic decoration. Thanks to his highly systematic approach to composition, Bridge realised the full implications of such harmony and developed it accordingly. *Ex 36a*, for instance, shows an important motive from the Piano Sonata's introduction. The chord sequence here might be explained as a piquant chain of dominant discords. But to Bridge the interval content of the chords suggested opposed tonalities: triads underpinned by alien seconds. *Ex 36b*, from the slow movement, shows how such chordal entities reverberated in his mind, and produced more explicit bitonal procedures.

While notably broadening his harmonic perspectives, Bridge realised the need for a renewal of structural thought to match the loosening of tonal bonds. The first movement of the Piano Sonata is in arch-shaped sonata form — another offshoot of the phantasy principle which had also influenced the Cello Sonata's first movement, but the phrase structure no longer flows with the old smoothness: it is splintered in a way that ideally embodies the fractured tonal vocabulary.

Occasionally the chromatic manner of an earlier Bridge emerges to suggest a past beyond recall, producing in the slow movement one of the most poignant phrases in all his work, a magically still centre round which the sonata's storms rage (*Ex 37*). The integration of such music with more

Ex. 37
Andante espressivo

advanced elements is superbly managed, and in the finale Bridge embarks on an heroic and gritty march which sometimes recalls Ireland at his grimmest, while making far more astringent use of fourth chords and bitonal combinations. The effect of the sonata is bitter and plangent, and its dedication to a young composer killed in the war, Ernest Farrer, hints perhaps at the source of Bridge's new-found expressive power.

Final harvest

Third String Quartet establishes total break with the past, relates to Second Viennese School while retaining a strong personal tone — *There is a willow* explores twilight world typical of late-Bridge — *Enter Spring*, formal proportions not entirely successful but proves the late style capable of a brighter vision, recalls earlier 'English' manner — darker forces prevail in *Trio Rhapsody, Second Piano Trio*, a completely individual masterpiece, and *Violin Sonata* — A new classicism and gritty optimism mark *Fourth String Quartet*, one of Bridge's greatest works, and perhaps his most radical — *Divertimenti* confirm Bridge's classical trend.

The sonata is a considerable work in its own right, and it points the way to Bridge's subsequent music, both in its intensely troubled feeling and in many aspects of its style and technique. The retention of certain elements of Bridge's previous vocabulary prevents the sonata from achieving a total break with the past, that achievement belongs to the Third String Quartet; but this should not be seen in negative terms, for, as was suggested above, those elements perform a precise expressive function, and a similar technical and stylistic point is made in *Enter Spring*, a work composed after the new style had been firmly established. The Piano Sonata might still belong in essence to the poetic world of Bax and Ireland, but it attempts far more in terms of language and syntax than either of those composers would have wanted to. In a less daring composer it might have marked the furthest distance its composer was prepared to travel within an accepted tradition, and have furnished him with an adequate vocabulary for the rest of his life. With Bridge it was a stepping stone, and after its completion he embarked on a series of chamber and orchestral masterpieces in which he found complete release. Their harmonic language and structural precepts can be related distantly to Scriabin, and more positively to Berg and Bartok, and they severed Bridge almost entirely from his English contemporaries at a time of firmly entrenched conservatism.

The first work to show Bridge's late manner in full flight, all impurities filtered out, the implications of his recently framed ideas completely realised, is the Third String Quartet, completed in 1926 — music which approaches the world of the Second Viennese School in its radical pro-

Ex. 38
Allegro moderato

cedures, while remaining utterly personal in tone. The first movement's first subject (*Ex 38*) is typical of the kind of energetic lyricism in which the quartet abounds: the sense of linear growth is as strong as ever, but the subtle web of tensions which binds the dislocated phrases together is far removed from the old flowing *cantabile*, as is the way in which all 12 chromatic notes are kept in play.

In the vertical aspects of his textures, Bridge approaches a Schoenbergian pantonality, but the lack of semitonal dissonance in the chord spacing and the tendency to select whole-tone and dominant formations gives an individual flavour. Harmonies of this kind are found in the middle-period works, but the speed with which they are now juxtaposed, and the freedom of the linear writing, dictate a totally different logic and create a new sound-world. The harmonic texture is further extended by the introduction of less orthodox chord structures. The superimposition of tritones and fourths favoured by the Viennese school becomes a new characteristic, as do tense Bartokian chords formed from interlocking major and minor thirds.

The structure of the Quartet's three movements shows an increasing richness and complexity of thought. Main material often appears after a period of assembly and preparation. For instance, *Ex 38* follows a nine-bar *andante* introduction and a further nine bars of motive-juggling. Formally, the whole work is dominated by modifications of the sonata principle — arch-shaped in the first movement, and with a rondo refrain in the finale. (It is indicative of the fertility of Bridge's invention that the abundance of material in the finale still leaves room for additional development of the main first-movement themes.) An examination of the microstructure of the quartet reveals startling facts for an English work of the 1920s. Like Schoenberg before him, Bridge realised the significance of a pervasive motive working as a support for developing argument in the absence of orthodox tonality, and extended the principle to the point of integrating vertical and horizontal aspects of the music. The quartet's opening melodic motive (x in *Ex 39a*), for example, in which the tritone and fifth above the initial B flat are sounded, suggests the two harmonic possibilities fourth supporting or (by inversion) supported by a tritone, transpositions of which immediately appear in the inner parts of bars 5 and 6, and are a prime constituent throughout the work. A transposition

Ex. 39a

of x also supplies a skeletonic outline of the crucial motive C-E flat — G-F sharp (w in *Ex 39a* and *Ex 38* — bar 2) and, through it, of the bitonal combination of triads, minor with major a tone higher (v in *Ex 39a*), which suffuses the harmonic texture of the quartet. (This chord is, in fact, an obsession with Bridge and figures prominently in nearly all his late works.)

Tracing the motive connections between successive phrases and incidents in the work, one is irresistibly reminded of the tightly packed motive development in pre-12-note works by Schoenberg and Berg. We can best see how Bridge's mind worked by comparing the exposition of motives (*Ex 39a*) which precedes the first subject with a tracery of some of the events in the development section (*Ex 39b*). Of special interest is the rearrangement of the scale pattern y in the motive z, indicating a permutational view of material, also the fact that its scale is founded on the fifth and tritone (A-D sharp-E).

Ex. 39b
Allegro

The elaborately figured and combative energy of the Third Quartet's outer movements, and the sad, uneasy half-lights of its central intermezzo inform nearly all the works of Bridge's maturity. But in the next major work to be completed, the darker expressive world is isolated for an intense exploration. *There is a Willow Grows Aslant a Brook* (1927) is scored for a chamber orchestra of single wind (plus second clarinet), harp and Strings and is a miracle of resourceful and atmospheric orchestration.

Growing out of the Queen's description of Ophelia's death in the Fifth Act of *Hamlet*, the form is highly original, and the work's haunted sonority is sustained without monotony, yet with hardly a glimmer of light, by the concentrated development of ideas exposed in the opening bars (*Ex 40*).

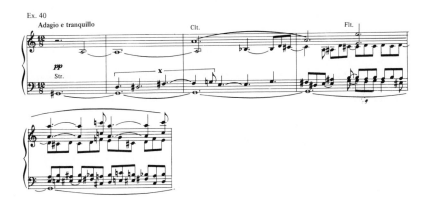

At the outset the little cell spawns long chains of notes by means of its interlocking major and minor thirds and semitones, yielding textures which somehow suggest both the wandering mind of Ophelia and the 'fantastic garlands ... weedy trophies'. This is the main section of a structure which combines elements of rondo and variation forms. The first interlude presents a plaintive rearrangement of the motive thirds — one of the 'old tunes' perhaps (*Ex 41*) — and after a return of the main material

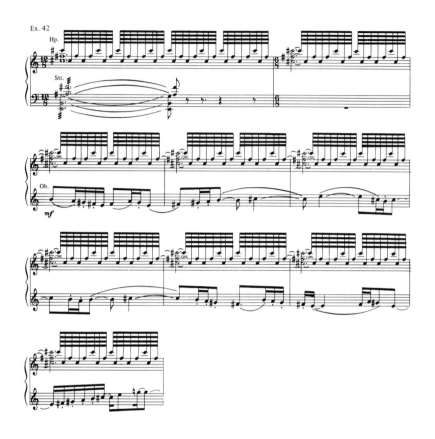

Ex. 42

in a developing variation, another song emerges (*Ex 42*). A psychological masterstroke, this, placing a flexible modal ditty of exquisite unpredictability in a most discreetly painful context, suggesting a wandering memory and an experience too wounding to recall. The score-reading eye has to take account of the E minor component of the bitonal harmony from which the accompaniment emerges, for its shadow colours the whole paragraph, even though its notes are extinguished before the tune arrives. After a passionately plaintive after-song on high strings, the clarinet, in frightening isolation, suggests 'down her weedy trophies and herself fell in the weeping brook'; and behind an intensified repeat of the main section — strings divisi, half tremolo *sul ponticello*, half muted, in watery gloom —

the 'snatches of old tunes' are heard, in effect a concentrated recapitulation of all the previous material before Ophelia is 'pull'd to her muddy death' (*Ex 43*). Motive x has already been discovered to outline the characteristic notes of Bridge's favourite bitonal chord, and now this becomes the accompaniment to a closing threnody on solo strings, itself saturated with the motive thirds (*Ex 44*). After this final flowering the inspired miniature sinks to its uneasy rest.

Enter Spring (1927), a tone poem for full orchestra, the composing of which Bridge interrupted to write *There is a Willow*, could not provide a greater contrast. It is the composer's most exuberant and untroubled masterpiece, and one of his grandest. After characteristic preliminaries, scintillatingly scored, the main thematic material begins to assemble itself, continually evolving what appear to be definitive statements only to move

77

Ex. 45

Ex. 46

on to further explorations. *Ex 45* shows one such stream of thought. Three motives, x, y and z, appear in constantly changing relationships while growing new offshoots; and the links in the process are separated by complementary developments.

After considerable development the music disolves for the moment into an enchanted interlude where fresh material is evolved in an apparently decorative flute solo which sings and dances with improvisatory freedom against a magical haze of muted trumpets and string harmonics. This subject becomes increasingly assertive and crowns a section of prodigious energy and breadth, surging and trampling to a triumphant climax in combination with earlier material. The work now moves with calm grandeur into a central pastoral whose heart-stopping beauty has few equals in twentieth-century English music (*Ex 46*). After serene extensions, decorated by birdsong, which unfold over quietly pulsing harmonies, the music rises to a glowing peak; but at this point Bridge sets himself a structural problem by broadening the climax over a further two pages. The sense of achievement here is undeniable as the melody swings forward, supported by chiming chords in ceremonial triumph; but it places a considerable burden on the latter portions of the work which are planned to close with a crowning reappearance of the same processional. In the event, Bridge seems to make a rare structural miscalculation, and in performance this final gesture gives an inflated impression. The intervening recapitulation of main-section material is so concentrated that the return of the striking processional music occurs too soon. It is strange that Bridge did not employ a structural procedure which had stood him in good stead at various times in his career, saving the climax of a thematic group for its recapitulation. All that was needed was to omit the two processional pages at the end of the central section. In this way he would have avoided anticipating the final climax and not overshadowed the repeat of the main section.

Apart from this question of proportion and structural emphasis, however, *Enter Spring* is a splendid achievement, showing how offshoots of Bridge's new language could embody a joyous vision. To do so he had to incorporate something of his earlier manner, but for Bridge the discovery of new expressive worlds never involved replacing old methods: he grew by adding rather than replacing, and the fact that the unclouded and perhaps less radical statement of *Enter Spring* followed the forward-looking *Third Quartet* is a salutary reminder that no composer's development of style is predictable, even with such an orderly artist as Bridge.

79

Enter Spring was nevertheless the last work in which he was to refer to the romanticism of his middle years, and in, for instance, the three chamber works that followed it — the *Rhapsody-Trio* (1928), Second Piano Trio (1929) and Violin Sonata (1932) — dark, emotionally ambivalent forces dominate the music.

The *Rhapsody-Trio*, for two violins, and viola, shows Bridge's mastery of string sonority at its height, and articulates a private and elusive world which contrasts with the grandeur of statement in the Piano Trio and Violin Sonata. The motive working is no less tight here than in the Third Quartet or *There is a Willow*, the utmost economy of thought giving an impression of rich profusion, and Bridge continues his preoccupation with interlocking major and minor thirds (x in *Ex 47*). A short introduction sets out two basic types of material, quick and slow, both spectral in mood (*Ex 47a* and *b*), and there follows a main section of energetically lyrical counterpoint, the two main groups, in what is in effect a seamless flow of music, permeated with motives from the introduction (*Ex 48*). The slow central section, in which the motive thirds eventually assume a more conventionally scalic form, becomes intensely inward, wonderfully personalised by Bridge's command of colour and textural spacing, and after a brief development the main subjects return in their original order — not reversed, as in the typical Bridge arch-form (for this is a phantasy in all but name and the composer's most concentrated example). All that remains is for the coda to return the music to the ghostly region of the opening, and there the work evaporates. At no point has the restricted com-

Ex. 47a

Ex. 47b

Ex. 48

pass of the music limited its emotional scope; indeed, it is turned to great expressive account, and the Trio numbers with Bridge's most subtle and individual creations, as many-sided in its way as more ambitious achievements.

In the *Rhapsody Trio*, Bridge uncovers deeper layers of his musical soul. If parts of the Third Quartet reveal, for all his independence of mind, an allegiance with the Second Viennese School, the Trio inhabits an unprecedented world. The individuality of vision which made such a work possible now expanded magnificently to produce the masterpiece which confirms Bridge as a composer of international stature, the Second Piano Trio. This Olympian work is laid out on the broadest lines, consisting, unusually for Bridge, of a pair of interlinked movements. Once again, the evolution of the melodic lines depends on characteristically related major and minor thirds, and again this idea is expressed vertically in terms of bitonally combined triads, the first two movements concentrating on linear expansion, the third on harmonic and the finale on tieing together previous developments.

At the outset Bridge launches a magnificently sustained flight of lyrical counterpoint, offsetting the tight corners in his searching melodic lines with the piano's open fifths (*Ex 49*). As so often in this work, and throughout late Bridge, it is easy to demonstrate the compositional mastery behind a process, but not the sheer individuality of the sonority and the thinking, whose rarified passion is difficult to relate to any other composer.

Ex. 51

Ex. 52

A marvellously intensified counterstatement, coming to earth after the stratospheric opening, reminds us with a shock how far Bridge had travelled since the *Phantasy Piano Trio*'s exposition and counterstatement over a keyboard ostinato. The bitonal aspects of the work's ubiquitous thirds come to the fore in the middle section, where a wandering theme (*Ex 50*) banishes all feeling of time with a chain of passacaglia-like repetitions and variations, continuing the discreet *allegretto* of the opening. The recapitulation builds to a majestic climax, where, after an allusion to the middle section, Bridge with consummate timing releases the vast accumulation of tension over a mere eight bars of explosive *allegro*. The movement ascends into a serenity that can only be compared with the Holst of *Betelgeuse*. The linked scherzo wrings fresh shapes from the pattern of thirds (*Ex 51*), and develops the idea of ostinato repetition to a machine-like pitch. We feel that, faced with an experience too painful to articulate, emotions freeze over and automatic processes aid the afflicted sensibilities. There is an interlude theme (*Ex 52*) in which the piano's right hand superimposes a more relaxed, quasi-modal line of thirds over the original tighter shape, and the centre of the movement (the trio, perhaps) is taken up with an expansive new melodic paragraph replete with motive thirds (*Ex 53*) — all these ideas punctuated and carried forward by the *scherzando* figures (*Ex 53*).

We are drawn even deeper into the aftermath of some searing experience in the haunting slow movement. Again there is the endless ticking

Ex. 53

of an ostinato rhythm, decked out now with rich bitonal harmony (*Ex 54a*). The main section is built from a sequence of little harmonic cells, each constructed from one of two bitonal combinations: minor triad with major a tone higher (the 'Bridge chord'), or major and minor sharing the same mediant. In the short central episode, part really of an unbroken span, the triads become augmented, combined only if they belong to the same whole-tone scale, and the melodic strands proliferate densely (*Ex 54b*).

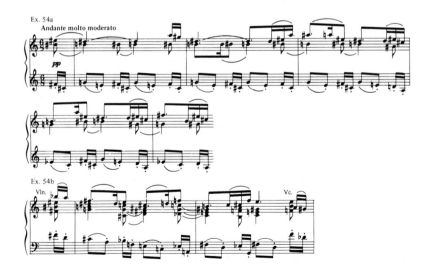

Ex. 54a
Andante molto moderato

Ex. 54b

Ex. 55

The finale weaves all these threads together in a sonata *allegro*. The opening subject (*Ex 55*) focusses on the 'Bridge chord', which supports a top line of characteristic thirds, and these thirds also permeate the second subject. Then, first-movement material combines with a subsidiary theme of the finale in the development which leads to a direct quotation of the trio's opening. This momentarily draws the music away from passionate engagement, but a return of the initial impetus brings with it the recapitulation, building a tumultuous climax which floods over into a restatement of the first movement's second theme. There is a sense of heroic attainment here, but the victory is hardly a comfortable one and the music withdraws poignantly to the heights it had occupied at the outset.

The Violin Sonata is hardly less impressive. Its single span goes much further than that of the *Rhapsody Trio* by embracing the four movements of traditional usage in sequence — sonata *allegro* exposition; *andante*; *scherzo*; recapitulation-cum-finale — yet integrating this apparently looser structure with the customary motive derivations. In no other work does Bridge pursue a more finely balanced course between freely burgeoning lyricism in line and harmony and the most tightly constructed development and variation of motive cells. The opening two bars, for example, are of the utmost significance motivically, exposing and developing the idea of interlocking major and minor thirds (*Ex 56a*), and hinting at the importance of tritonally related components in bitonal chords (*Ex 56b*), both of which are vital ingredients in the sonata's micro-structure. After the concentrated introduction, the *allegro* states the most important subject in the work (*Ex 57*), a theme whose head-motive influences harmonic

85

Ex. 56a

Ex. 56b

and melodic writing throughout the sonata. In the first bar there is a skeletal reference to the tritonal harmony of *Ex 56b*, isolating from it the component tritone plus fourth, typical of late Bridge; and the second bar exposes another chord structure (x) which will later produce sequences like *Ex 58x*. Finally, in the top line there is the all-important melodic fourth suspended on an axis of C sharp. The continuation of this subject shows how motive development and variation operates on a bar-by-bar basis throughout a melodic flight. Transitional material is related through its sevenths to the all-important fourths (*Ex 58y*), and also employs the interlocking thirds and the characteristic harmony of *Exx 56* and *57*. Tritones, fourths and interlocking thirds reassemble in fresh combinations at the start of the second main subject, which also refers, if distantly, to the headmotive (*Ex 59*).

The two middle movements evolve their own material from previous motives and also quote earlier subjects directly, yielding a tightly woven network of relationships. The *Andante*, for instance, opens with a theme that combines elements of the head motive and the interlocking thirds surrounded by harmony which is saturated by tritones and fourths (*Ex 60*). It proceeds to a passionate climax where the head motive returns to ride a flood of keyboard sound, and is then subjected to elaborately

86

Ex. 57

Allegro molto moderato

Ex. 58

Ex. 59

Poco tranquillo

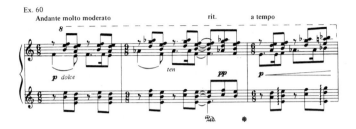

Ex. 60

decorated variation (*Ex 61*) before the opening material is recapitulated. *Ex 59* provides a link to the *scherzo*, which is again dominated by fourths and tritones (*Ex 62*). There are two little trios in what is an unbroken, headlong progress. Each opens with a short phrase drawn from the minor version of the head-motive, and then unfolds a first movement melody so far undeveloped — transitional material in the first interlude, the introductory theme in the second.

Ex. 61

Ex. 62

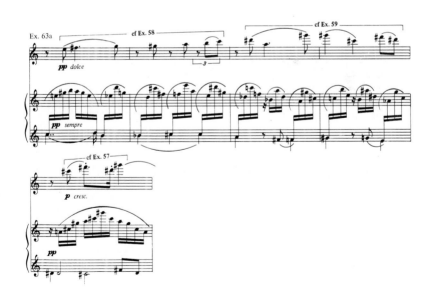

Ex. 63a

A further new combination alligning the slow-movement fourths with the sonata's introduction leads to the finale, where first-movement material is re-ordered, developed and intensified (*Ex 63*). It brings to a conclusion one of Bridge's most richly varied and powerful works, reaching back towards the *Third Quartet* in its energetically lyrical outer sections, and to something of the dead feeling behind the mechanistic writing in the *Second Piano Trio*, while making a uniquely personal gesture in the *Andante*, which is both passionately florid in its *cantabile*, yet also strangely detached in its schematic chord-building. Bridge's language was rarely more richly inclusive than in this work, making wholesale use of fourths and whole-tone harmony as well as the tried and trusted interlocking thirds, drawing at times on the old 'English' romanticism, reaching out also towards total chromaticism, and integrating all these elements perfectly to give an overall impression of stylistic purity.

Bridge's output of chamber music was completed by two characteristic works, the Fourth String Quartet (1937) and *Divertimenti* for wind quartet (1934–38). The string quartet, which marks perhaps the peak of his writing in the genre, resembles its predecessor in certain respects. There is a similar vein of lyrical energy to that shown in *Ex 38*, and the central movement is again a wistful intermezzo. But it is now in the finale that a slow introduction leads, via an assembly of motives, to a definitive thematic statement, and its rondo structure presses to a conclusion of hard-won optimism, contrasting with the melancholy into which the Third Quartet descends. In more general terms, the language has moved away from the expressionist richness of its predecessor: a more classical vision is outlined by the concentrated statements, concise transitions, and increased economy of texture. At the same time there is room enough for lyrical growth, and the first movement's second subject can afford counter-statements, albeit in varied forms, which remind us of Bridge's early expansive vein. There is also space for the obligatory references to the first-movement material as the work closes. In its harmonic world the Fourth Quartet is the most radical of all Bridge's works, and its preoc-cupation with the more open intervals — fourths, fifths, major thirds and ninths — gives a new textural personality, uncomprisingly dissonant and bracing (*Ex 64a*). The old obsession with interlocking thirds has left its mark, but the composer's harmonic resources are becoming increasing-ly wide-ranging, and the masterly way in which he saturates the texture of the finale with fifths, the interval of optimism and tonal orientation, using overtone structures to suggest a high norm of polytonal dissonance,

Ex. 64a

Allegro energico

Ex. 64b

Largamente

Ex. 65

Allegro con brio

typifies the new freedom (*Ex 65*).

The quartet's opening sonata structure is far more concise than its counterpart in the Third Quartet, yet it manages to encompass as many changes of pace, mood and texture, welding and integrating them through the fierce heat and energy of its compressed processes. Plunging immediately into a maelstrom of gritty, motivic activity, for instance (*Ex 64a*), it as quickly becomes subdued for a *largamente* transformation (*Ex 64b*) before launching out animatedly once more on transitional material. The formal compression is made possible by the extreme concentration of the motive work and the tight developmental web of the texture. *Ex 66* shows how cells grow during later stages of the movement, and gives some idea of how motives can saturate the whole texture at moments of determined contrapuntal growth. In common with the general terseness of thought, the working-out section proper is short and the recapitulation literal, apart from the omission of counterstatements and moments of expansion. This leaves the way clear for the coda to broaden the movement's formal horizon with two brief but unerringly judged processes — a further short development of first-subject material and a tender postlude which neatly balances the *largamente* treatment of the first subject in the exposition by similarly transforming the second subject.

If the intermezzo opens in a wistful vein like that of its counterpart in the Third Quartet, the mood is soon broken up by lively bursts of grotesquerie (*Ex 67*). In fact this quasi-menuetto, like much else in the work, is really without expressive precedent in Bridge's music; in common with certain movements in the Viennese classical repertory it combines toughness of thought with an apparently capricious and divertimento-like manner. The minuet and trio form, for instance, is enriched by sonata elements; there is the suggestion of a second subject in the main section (*Ex 68*), and the trio is a development of first subject and introductory material, while the recapitulation omits the second subject but richly extends and contrapuntally works the first, including a reference to the first movement's second subject (*Ex 69*). Finally, a compressed structure is subtly opened out by the little semiquaver phrases that link many of the paragraphs (*Ex 67x*), giving a sense of freedom and improvisatory leisure.

The finale is certainly one of Bridge's finest achievements, a fitting conclusion technically and emotionally to a great work. Typically its rondo form is of the utmost simplicity, A — B — A — B — A, which allows the two principle subjects of the first movement to be worked into the

Ex. 66
(cf Ex. 64 a & b, x, y & z)
Allegro energico

Ex. 67

Ex. 68

Ex. 69

transition to the final rondo statement without overburdening the structure. This brief return to the darker forces of the work's opening renders the rondo theme's final winging development the more impressive in its spiritual courage.

Divertimenti confirms Bridge's classical trend and develops his elusive, at times almost fugitive, manner. Although true to its title in scope of feeling, it is a toughly argued work, laconic in statement, and prone to neo-classical rhythmic contours. There are four movements, of which the middle two are duets, for flute and oboe, and clarinet and bassoon respectively. The first movement, which could be sub-titled 'Fanfare, Pastoral and Miniature March', reconciles perfectly the suite-like succession of ideas characteristic of the divertimento with a rigorous development of motive cells. The opening fanfare exposes a group of eight notes consisting of major thirds and their inversions linked by false relation (*Ex 70a*), and then briefly develops it. A little pastoral ensues, characterised

by fourths (giving a slightly Hindemithian flavour) and leading to a return of the opening bars. At this point a simply varied recapitulation might have been expected; but by means of thematic transformation Bridge launches an apparently new section, greatly extending the frontiers of the structure — a brief march which re-orders the content of the eight-note group (*Ex 70b*). References to the pastoral fourths provide a tiny

trio. The second movement, *Nocturne,* is in Bridge's haunted mood, a rather loose-limbed improvisatory piece, and the third, *Scherzetto,* is drily repetitive, the only dull music Bridge wrote in his maturity. Invention returns to normal in the final *Bagatelle,* however, producing a movement that hovers between skittish humour and something nearer to apprehensive flight.

The final orchestral works

Phantasm, a flawed conception but presents an English expressionist vision for which there are no precedents — *Oration*, perhaps Bridge's masterpiece, a monumental funeral address over the dead of the Great War — *Rebus*, Bridge's last complete work, establishes a new simplicity of form and language — unfinished *Symphony for Strings* leaves enigmatic impression — tragedy of Bridge's untimely death prevents him from establishing contact with the young post-war progressives — a figure who reconciled an advanced European language with an English vision.

The orchestral works from the final decade of Bridge's life were until comparatively recently unknown to all but a few musicians and enthusiasts. Two of them — *Oration* (1930) and *Rebus* (1940) — were only recently published, in 1979 and 1978 respectively, while the third, *Phantasm* for piano and orchestra (1931), has only ever been available as a two-piano score. Each is a work of unmistakeable presence, and *Phantasm* is perhaps the easiest to relate to the music so far discussed for, as its title suggests, it explores the twilight world so dear to Bridge. The elaborate ternary form unfolds after an improvisatory introduction which defines the basic premises and (despite a long solo '*quasi improvisando*') establishes the piano in an atmospheric and decorative role rather than as the traditional protagonist of a concerto. Dream-like images are suggested by prominent melodic tritones and whole-tonal and bitonal textures, and a nightmarish feeling begins to take over as a result of the strange motion of the *allegro*. Continuous semi-quavers on the piano (and occasionally in the orchestra) give the impression of running while remaining rooted to the spot, and lend a weird significance to the main theme (*Ex 71a*) which arrives, dark on the bassoons, after a typical period of motivic assembly. It is related to the pastoral shape of *Enter Spring*'s central melody, but the piano's relentless ostinato throws a haunted light on this image of the past. After a counterstatement, with the piano in parallel open fifths, the tutti further distorts the theme with bitonal polyphony, the persistent semi-quavers now prominently high in the texture (*Ex 71b*), and a *scherzando* second group capriciously transforms the material of the atmospheric introduction, concentrating on its falling tritones G-C sharp, and D sharp-A. The central section moves through an eerie dreamscape, evolving fresh

Ex. 71a

Ex. 71b

combinations from the same material (*Ex 72*) while also extending it and introducing a new chant-like melody. The recapitulation is comparatively orthodox, but prepares the way for a climactic fulfilment of the principle of nightmarish distortion. *Ex 71a*, becoming increasingly insistent, erupts on full brass over battering timpani, while octave Ds on wind and strings mark the down-beats. The vision is intensified by the addition of a single contrapuntal strand on the tuba, after which the music subsides into the mysterious depths from which it arose.

Phantasm is not an unflawed work. Particularly, the piano writing seems in some respects to have been misconceived. The introduction, for example, is extended beyond its thematic or even atmospheric use to the main structure by the relaxed repetitions of rather idly arpeggiated piano textures. If this was a concerto proper, then elaborate and fanciful cadenza work would certainly be in place at this point — Brahms's Second Piano

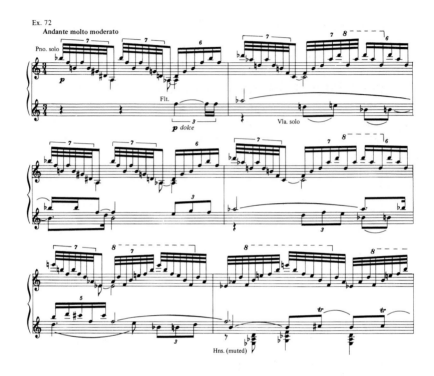

Concerto provides an honourable precedent; but as it is, there is little of display or soloistic individuality in the writing, which precludes the possibility of concerto duality, of the dramatic interplay vital to the genre. Given the decorative nature of the piano's role, all tendencies to wander cadenza-like should have been firmly checked. The middle section's 'chant' provides another cause for concern, for it seems to sit rather uneasily in its surroundings. The sequential extensions of its foursquare shape are something of a cliché, and the harmonic ambience of its parallel fourths and major thirds seems out of place.

There is, nevertheless, considerable breadth of vision, defined by simple themes, sometimes weirdly distorted, as well as by totally chromatic textures and lines; and the work as a whole presents a quite extraordinary poetry, struck with a haunted beauty, bizarre and sometimes fearful. It seems almost as if Bridge has created here a brand of English expressionism for which there are no precedents.

Oration counterbalances this expression of the darker side of Bridge's nature. Monumental in its power and thematic energy, rather than poetically atmospheric or expressionist, it is nevertheless suffused with the emotional ambivalence of Bridge's mature thought. While appearing to be public in its rhetoric and sense of solemn celebration, it belongs in a deeper sense to a private world, and the opposition of cello — that most speaking and, at times, inward of instruments — and orchestra perfectly embodies this concept. The work is, in fact, a funeral address over the lost of the 1914 – 18 war, and contrasts a deep personal grief with occasional grandeur and images of war. It is by implication a passionate indictment.

Formally, it is quite distinct from *Phantasm*, for it owes nothing to the symphonic poem design but is the last and grandest example of Bridge's phantasy arch-from. The work provides countless examples of the composer's flexible motive development, and much of its material is drawn from the opening of its expansive introduction (*Ex 73a*): the constituent

Ex. 73a

Ex. 73b

Ex. 73c

thirds of the triads bound by false relation are of paramount importance, as can be seen from the beginning of both the first and second subjects of the main section (*Ex 73b* and *c*). The chief elements of the introduction are a long solo recitative supported by *Ex 73 a*'s triads, and a processional, also built from the triads, over a wrong-note ground bass. March-like images figure prominently in the work's ceremonial atmosphere, and the central section, which is loosely developmental, consists of a bizarre march, as of platoons of the dead, underpinned by the timpani's persistent four-in-a-bar on a pedal G. The cello's capricious tune is taken over by two piccolos and oboe, producing a fife-like ostinato against which the first subject is recalled.

The main section and its recapitulation come nearer to traditional concerto concepts than does *Phantasm*: the first subject, energetically stated and extended by the soloist, leads to a powerfully contrapuntal tutti, and the second group shares material between cello and orchestra. The order of subjects, true to the principles of the phantasy sonata arch, is reversed upon recapitulation, and the second theme follows immediately on the heels of the receding march of the middle section. After a short cello cadenza the first group, greatly concentrated, brings a resurgence of energy — indeed, a continuation of development, for the contrapuntal activity is increased, and the second theme is drawn into the polyphonic fabric. At this point the introductory processional returns in full orchestral panoply, and the work's initial triads eventually die away, apparently closing the arch-form. However, there follows an unexpectedly long and haunting epilogue: 55 bars of sparsely textured *andante* threaded on an unbroken harp ostinato. Here the work enters a new expressive area, calm yet withdrawn in its mourning, which greatly expands the imaginative scope of an already spacious masterpiece.

Oration is one of the pinnacles not only of Bridge's art but of 20th-century British music. Indeed, it can be placed with the finest orchestral works of the first half of the century, for in its inspired blend of the unpredictable with the logical and orderly, in its perfection of utterance, and in its large-scale control of contrasting tensions, it bears the hall-mark of a classic.

Bridge's last completed work, the overture *Rebus*, strikes out unpredictably on a new path, not, as one might have expected, drawing on the radical harmonic and thematic style established in the Fourth Quartet, for the forward-looking tendencies of Bridge's mature thought nearly always found their most concentrated and uncompromising expression in the chamber music. On the contrary, what is special to *Rebus* is the way in which characteristically rigorous motive operations are carried out on a much simpler, tonal idea. The work was originally to have been called *Rumour*, until Bridge realised that the war had lent the word sinister overtones, since the principle expressive idea is of a theme which is progressively varied and distorted, as it is passed from instrument to instrument. Appropriately what evolves is a monothematic sonata structure, everything of importance stemming from the opening three bars (*Ex 74a*). Some of the most important stages in its transformation are indicated in *Ex 74b* from later in the introduction, in *74c* from the first subject, d from the second, e from the development, and f, the coda.

Ex. 74a

Ex. 74b

Ex. 74c

After more than a decade of inward-looking music that had increasingly estranged him from his public, Bridge was clearly attempting a greater directness and simplicity of utterance in *Rebus*. The unclouded and triumphant C major of the second subject, for example, is unprecedented in his late years (*Ex 74d*). In reconciling such flowing statements with the elliptical and dislocated phraseology found in, say, the coda, a texturally attenuated section with sudden pauses and abrupt punctuation, Bridge shows his customary mastery. The essentially extravert and

103

ultimately compromising gesture of *Rebus* may have pointed to new departures. But if one is to speculate on what Bridge — ever the explorer — might have achieved had he not died a year later, still in his early sixties and clearly at the height of his powers, one surely sees him building on the radical achievement of the Fourth Quartet, combining breadth of style with concision.

In fact some slight confirmation of this prognostication was provided when the unfinished *Symphony for Strings* came to light in the mid-1970s. It had not been lost, but was languishing in the Bridge collection at the Royal College of Music, where to date it had roused no great interest. This is the music Bridge had been working on the day he died, and considering that he had long contemplated but so far not attempted a symphony, the title indicates the importance he must have attached to the project. The music that has come down to us consists of 358 bars in full score and a fairly explicit sketch for a closing 20-bar coda, which has been realised by Anthony Pople. It is this version which has been used in all the performances so far and in the first commercial recording. The *Allegro Moderato*, as it has come to be called, will always be an enigmatic piece, for we cannot know what was to follow, and later music would have been of crucial importance to our understanding of what is, by Bridge's standards, a loose-limbed opening movement. It palpably ends on a half close, and further spans would assuredly have tightened the structural knot and introduced contrasted material and tempos. In this respect it can not be said to relate to the Fourth Quartet; but it does share with that work a certain simplicity of statement, as it does a harmonic world dominated by fourths and fifths and a strong tendency for melodic lines to gravitate to interlocking thirds as well as, again, fourths and fifths. The tightly constructed contrapuntal networks of the quartet are not present, but such an essentially chamber-music technique is hardly suited to the orchestral symphony, and the motive development is more leisurely in style. The *Allegro Moderato* is nevertheless deeply serious, even monumental in expression, and at the impressive if brief dying fall which closes it we feel strongly that tensions have yet to be resolved, or indeed fully stated.

Bridge returns in this, his last work, to what had been a life-long preoccupation with the sonata arch, and launches an exposition of considerable spaciousness. There are three main subject groups, of which the first (*Ex 75a, b, c*) and third (*Ex 75e*) are little ternary structures; and a plethora of clearly-marked themes are presented, all sharing the identity imposed by fourths or interlocking thirds (*Ex 75*). We have, in fact, regressed to earlier days, when Bridge would launch a leisurely exposition in phantasy structures, and after flowing lyrical extensions find development difficult or else avoid it altogether. In the *Allegro Moderato* the development is short and flows easily out of the third subject (*Ex 76*), producing music which is perhaps rather too similar in kind to the broad exposition. It is at this point that the work begins to sound positively un-symphonic, which makes

105

Ex. 75e

Ex. 76

Tranquillo

etc.

the prospect of possible subsequent movements the more tantilizing. At a late stage in the recapitulation the balance is somewhat redressed when part of the third subject is developed in earnest, producing a short but fiery *Allegro deciso*. But the movement as a whole can not help but leave us in a state of expectation.

In coming years it may be seen as a tragedy for English music that Bridge was not allotted another 15 years of full creative vigour. Apart from greatly enriching the chamber music and orchestral repertories, he would have lived on into an era where he would have connected with a less hide-bound generation of musicians, the only senior figure who had faced up to the most advanced continental developments and proved that an English composer of integrity could emerge from the experience not only unscathed but immeasurably enriched.

INDEX

Allegro moderato, 105

Canzonetta, 66
Cello Sonata, 45
Cherry Ripe, 67
Christmas Rose, The, 48

Dance Rhapsody, 35
Dance Poem, 36
Day After Day, 68
Dedication, A, 66
Divertimenti, 96
Dweller in my Deathless Dreams, 68

Enter Spring, 77

Fairy Tale, A, 65
First String Quartet, 19
Four Characteristic Pieces, 65
Fourth String Quartet, 91

Gargoyle, 66
Go Not, Happy Day, 68
Graziella, 66

Hidden Fires, 66
Hour Glass, The, 65

Idylls, 20
In Autumn, 66
Into Her Keeping, 68
Isabella, 28

Last Invocation, The, 68
Love Went A'riding, 68

Miniature Pastorals, 65

Noveletten, 20

Oration, 101

Phantasm, 98
Phantasy Piano Trio, 15
Phantasy Piano Quartet, 15

Phantasy String Quartet, 15
Piano Quintet, 23
Piano Sonata, 69
Prayer, A., 45

Rebus, 102
Rhapsody-Trio, 80

Sally In Our Alley, 67
Sea, The, 25
Second Piano Trio, 81
Second String Quartet, 41
Sir Roger de Coverley, 67
So Perverse, 68
Speak To Me, My Love, 68
Strew No More Red Roses, 68
String Sextet, 24
Suite for Strings, 29
Summer, 39
Symphony for Strings, 105

There Is a Willow Grows Aslant a
    Brook, 75
Third String Quartet, 71
Three Improvisations, 65
Three Lyrics, 65
Three Pieces, 65
Three Poems, 65
Three Sketches, 65
Thy Hand in Mine, 68
'Tis But a Week', 68
Two Poems, 40

Vignettes de Marseilles, 66
Vignette de Danse, 67
Violin Sonata, 85

What Shall I Your True Love Tell?, 68
When You Are Old, 68
Where She Lies Asleep, 68
Winter Pastoral, 66

APPENDIX

The Frank Bridge Trust

The Frank Bridge Trust, administered by the Royal College of Music, acts as a centre for information about Bridge and his music. It also gives grants to encourage performance of his larger works, sponsors gramophone recordings, books and other publications, and maintains an archive.

Its executive committee is Sir David Willcocks (chairman), A P Miller (treasurer), John Bishop (secretary), Lewis Foreman, Dr Trevor Bray, Paul Hindmarsh and Anthony Payne.

Available from the secretary — see address below — are leaflets giving full details of all of Bridge's music currently in print or available on gramophone records or cassettes.

Issued in 1983 by Faber Music, with financial support from the Bridge Trust, was *Frank Bridge: A Thematic Catalogue*. This comprehensive book, compiled by Paul Hindmarsh, gives details of all Bridge's works.

Frank Bridge: Radical and Conservative has been published with financial support from the Trust.

All enquiries should be addressed to:
John Bishop
Secretary, Frank Bridge Trust
14 Barlby Road
London W10 6AR
(01-969 3579)